AT THE OVERSEER'S DOOR

The story of

Suffolk's parish workhouses

Hadleigh

By

Ray Whitehand

Published by Historical Suffolk Publishing:
28 Lincoln Avenue, Saxmundham, Suffolk. IP17 1BZ

ISBN: 978-0-9555563-0-2

Typical parish workhouse

Printed by Lavenham Press, Arbon's House, Lavenham. CO10 9RN

AT THE OVERSEER'S DOOR

Illustrations and sketches:
Front cover plus black and white sketches courtesy of *Illustrated London News*,
available at Ipswich Record Office and at: *http://www.iln.org.uk/*
Back cover: *St Mary le Tower, Ipswich from sketch by E Pococke*

Chapter sketches:
chs. 1,3,5 & 8 drawn from pictures at: *http://www.workhouses.org.uk/*
ch 2. Little Cornard from: *S.R.O.(I) J1/11/1/3*
ch. 4, Brandon from: *www.brandon-heritage.co.uk*
ch. 6, Blaxhall from: *S.R.O.(I) K681/1/44/7*
ch. 7, Framlingham from various sources.

Maps
Inside front and back cover: by the editor

Photographs between pages: 46 & 47
i: *Brandon Town Book, S.R.O.(B) FL536/7/1*
ii: *Memorandum of Requirements of the Workhouse; Framlingham Overseers
Accounts. S.R.O.(I) FC101/G19/7*
iii: *The Ipswich Journal 23rd February 1782*
iv: *Metfield Overseers S.R.O.(I) FC91/G11/1*
v: *Brandon Town Book S.R.O.(B) FL536/7/1*
vi: *Assington Building costs, S.R.O.(B) FL521/7/10*
vii: *Fire Insurance policy 1803; & premium receipt for Groton workhouse 1789-
1826; S.R.O.(B); FL506/7/38*
viii: *Hadleigh workhouse 'Contract Book' 1789-1809; S.R.O.(B); FB81/G1/1*

Acknowledgements:
This volume would not have been possible without the help of a number of individuals
who have assisted and advised on matters such as research, editing, proofing and
layout, including the staff of the three Suffolk Record Offices, whose assistance and
tolerance with my numerous queries have been substantial. However any errors or
misinterpretations are accepted as the responsibility of the author himself.

18th century peasant family

FOREWORD

The following was found in Earl Stonham parish chest; written by a Justice of the Peace to one of the overseers of the parish: *S.R.O.(I) FB23/G4/1*

This woman the bearer hereof beinge l*[ef]*t*[?]* widowed by her husband w*[i]*th child, & havynge uncharytble dealynge by her neybors, hath complayned to the Justices at o*r* last sess*[ion]*s at Jpswyche, who takynge pytty on the poore womans estate moved you as one of the overseers of the poore \beinge then present/ to provide for her a dwellynge place in yo*[u]*r towne, w*[hi]*ch motion of our (as J remember) you yelded unto, & promised to p*[er]*forme, & therefore J marvayle she should nowe complayne agayne,

Wherfore J thought good to wryt to you \to/ desire you to doe that w*[hi]*ch you \ar/ bound as overseers to doe, for yo*r* offyce is to make provision of 3 sorts of poore, that is to say \first/ maynteynance for the aged sycke & impotent \that cannot worke/, second punishement in the howse of correccon for *[damage]* Jdle poore that wyll not worke & thyrd *[damage]* worke, for the wyllynge poore to worke & cannot gett worke; this poore woman is one of this last sort, who is wyllynge to worke, but she cannot worke w*[i]*thout a Rowme or place to worke in, & that is where she may shrowd herselfe in, this roome you ar to provyd for her, as a matter required of you by vertue of yor offyce; th*[a]*t you doe th*[a]*t not, you must thynke ther be lawes that wyll requyre the penalty at yor hands for neglect of yor dewty herein

Th*[a]*t you say you cannot gett a howse or a Rowme for her, that is noe excuse for by the leave you ar to erect & set up a cottage upon the wast ground in yor towne, w*[i]*th the consent of the Lord of the manor.
[Next page]

Yf the Lord wyll not consent you ar to complayne to the Justices of peace who ar to treat w*[i]*th the Lord but in the meane tyme you may not suffer the poore to be destitute.

J pray consyder of this poore woman & lett us not heare suche complaynts as heretofore hathe byn heared consyder the necessyty of the poore woman beinge destitute of her husbands helpe.

you may perceyve that \by/ the scantnes of paper J dyd not thynke to wryt so lardgly to you when J began to wryt as I have donne but after J began, the more J wrott, the mor I thought the cause of the poore woman to be pyttyed, & therfore you must take th[a]t (as J doe) that Gods *[damage]* is in yt, & therefore J pray *[damage]* not slyghtly regard this my desyre th*[a]*t is noe pryvate matter, but hath byn publyquely herd in the Sess*[ions]* & therefore \yf/ you neglect your dewty herein, yor fault wyll not be pryvate but publyque. But J hope you wyll regard this w*[hic]*h J have wrytten & so J com*[me]*nd you to god. 22 of J*[?]*e 1622 by yor freynd

Robte Vigerous

==========

5

18th century carters

Chapter One

AN OVERVIEW

Westhorpe

We learn from our history books of the degree of effort our ancestors have made to care for the less fortunate of our society. From medieval times and beyond, there has always been the recognition of a need to reach out and help certain groups genuinely unable to help themselves.

It is the definition of 'genuine' which has caused much debate and contention. In medieval times attitude towards the less able was one of acceptance. The gentry were content to accept the poor and needy as a part of the social structure of the time. Equally most poor were content with their lot. Expectation was everything and nothing! What could not be tolerated was the idle poor and beggars. Even Edward VI himself retorted 'the vagabond ought clearly to be banished from our land'[1].

'Grinding poverty' brought about by the likes of the Black Death was estimated by early Elizabethan times to affect as much as half of the country. While parliament was willing to legislate against those despised beggars and vagabonds,[2] any assistance for the

7

genuine needy was left to individuals and charities, with religious bodies playing a significant role. Following the dissolution of the monasteries in 1536, something which significantly contributed to a fragmentation of the medieval social structure; provision for the caring of the poor moved from a voluntary basis to a more compulsory system of taxation in the form of poor rates.

During the reign of Queen Elizabeth I, the amount of poverty in the country finally reached such epidemic proportions it became clear something had to be done. Depression in the national textile industry, changes within agriculture and an expanding population had all served to feed an ever-spiralling growth in unemployment. Rural counties such as Suffolk were particularly hard hit.

Agricultural labourers now took to the roads in their hundreds in a desperate attempt to find work, leaving their wives and families behind. They knew failure to find employment could result in a life of existence amongst the down and outs and vagabonds. The family left behind would go cap in hand to local charities for help. As mentioned above, providing for the most needy, the old, sick and disabled at this period of time was still seen as the responsibility of religious and charitable establishments. Aid was usually provided in the form of 'out relief', with clothing, food, firewood or financial assistance being given to paupers in their own homes[3].

In the second half of the sixteenth century a national attempt was made to control this increasing problem. Parliament created a series of Poor Relief Acts. The first in 1564[4], targeted the 'roaming beggars' by authorizing parish officers to *'appoint meet and convenient places for the habitations and abidings of such classes*; the first inference to a workhouse. A further Act in 1597[5] saw the appointment of an unpaid supervisor in each parish to oversee the care and maintenance of its poor; hence the Parish Overseer was born. This was followed in 1601[6] by *An Acte for the Reliefe of the Poor.* This sought to identify and separate the 'deserved poor' from the vagrants and layabouts.

The first parish workhouses in Suffolk appeared in the larger towns. Hadleigh and Ipswich had both set aside buildings for this use by 1575[7]. The workhouse at Hadleigh was so successful it was highlighted as an example of what could be achieved, in a report which pre-empted the 1601 Act. The three primary elements of this Act were: 1) To seek to bring up unprotected children in habits of industry'; 2) To provide work for those capable, but unable to find any; 3) To provide materials such as flax, hemp and wool as a means of employment for those able bodied poor. The intention was to provide a safety net for the *'the deserved poor'*. Responsibility for the administration of this relief was placed in the hands of the local parish officers, with the newly appointed overseer, the head person. Any necessary costs were to be borne out by an obligatory poor rate levied on the majority of householders.

The gradual decline of the 'old draperies' trade, which began in the latter years of the Elizabethan period, became a significant factor in the growth of unemployment here in Suffolk. Particularly hard hit were the towns and villages in the Babergh and Cosford hundreds[8]. These districts had enjoyed the fruits of the industry during its heyday, particularly from the mid fifteenth into the early part of the sixteenth century. Towns like Sudbury, Lavenham and Hadleigh still show off properties built in this golden period, and funded by the production of some of the best broadcloths, kerseys and worsteds in the land. By the end of the 1500s towns and parishes alike felt the sharp tongue of the depression which covered much of the country.

The combination of a loss of overseas trade, coupled with an increase of imports of 'new draperies' from France and Holland added significant impetus to the decline[9]. Whole families which had eked out a living spinning, weaving, dyeing and fulling, suddenly found themselves unable to afford the most basic of essentials. Once major contributors to the local economy, many of these family-run businesses which had been handed down from generation to generation, now became insolvent. Their isolation and smallness meant they were unable to survive in a dramatically changing industry.

Throughout the seventeenth century as the numbers of paupers grew all over the country, so the concept of the parish workhouse took off as a means of controlling the problem. Hearth Tax returns of 1674 suggest as much as half the population of some parishes was classified as poor[10]. The workhouse was one of the premises exempt of this duty[11]. Slowly more and more vestries tried out this new method of managing the poor. In most cases these parish workhouses were no more than ordinary labourer's cottages, acquired from a range of sources. Town houses were often utilised. Wealthy property owners would make an endowment either as a lifetime gift or as a bequest in their Will. Some of the larger, once wealthy textile towns like Lavenham and Hadleigh, had old decaying medieval Guild Halls, remnants of their heydays. Now redundant as a result of the dissolution of Henry VIII, these were, in some cases, repurchased from the crown and brought back into local use.

In 1722 an Act of Parliament[12] which became known as Knatchbull's Act after the politician chiefly responsible for its creation; made further significant directives to those responsible for the management of the Poor. Firstly and probably most contentiously, it gave parishes the option of refusing 'out relief'. Instead in order to obtain relief paupers had to be admitted into the workhouse. It was thought this would deter all but the most desperate from applying, and thereby contain the amount of relief required from ratepayers. Secondly it allowed parishes to unite in order to provide a workhouse for their poor. By spreading the costs of running these establishments it was felt it would lessen the burden on the smaller parishes who found the cost of a workhouse unsustainable. Furthermore parishes now only had to get the consent of the majority of its parishioners, followed by the approval of the local Justice of the Peace, rather than apply for a specific Act of Parliament in order to set up a workhouse, as had previously been the case[13].

Another aspect of Knatchbull's Act was the introduction of 'farming out'. Instead of a parish undertaking the administration of the workhouse and its inmates, they were now able to contract out parts of the maintenance of their poor to a third party. Parish officers would invite tenders from suitably qualified persons to take charge of elements of their poor. This might take the form of responsibility for the management of the poor of the whole parish or merely that of the day-to-day running of the workhouse, together with its inmates and their employment. In return for this, a lump sum and / or a weekly rate per inmate would be offered. Profits from the employment carried out in the workhouse may also be included in the package as an incentive. Interested persons would be invited to tender their best offer for the position to the overseers of the parish.

To demonstrate the growth of the parish workhouse in the early eighteenth century, the Society for Promoting Christian Knowledge published *'An Account of several Workhouses for employing and maintaining the Poor'*. The first edition in 1725 named 126 establishments nationally, while a second edition just seven years later added a further fifty five to the directory[14]. In 1776 a national survey carried out for Parliament to identify the location and size of all parish workhouses in the country identified ninety four such premises in Suffolk alone[15].

The parish workhouse initially proved reasonably successful in containing the poverty issue. Even so the management of the poor remained the biggest problem facing parish officers. By the middle part of the eighteenth century a significant element of the gentry, including magistrates, affluent farmers, and prosperous tradesmen had became concerned about the overall state of affairs. For a variety of reasons more and more paupers were becoming in need of relief of one form or other. Conscious of what was happening across the water in France, where peasants had risen against the 'authority' in violent rebellion; this influential sector of 'principal inhabitants' sought to prevent the same things happening this side of the channel[16].

Meetings and gatherings took place all over the country in an attempt to identify how best to deal with this increasing problem. One idea, which met with broad appeal, was for the merger of large groups of parishes to form 'Incorporations' designed to oversee the whole issue of Poor Law within their district. By spreading the cost of maintaining the poor over a greater number of parishes it was felt a better more cost effective regime could be had. This led to the creation of a number of Incorporations. Based roughly on the ancient hundredal divisions, these newly formed amalgamations took on the mantle of poor law management of all the parishes which fell within their catchment area, on average numbering between twenty and thirty. These incorporations proceeded to build enormous workhouses capable of holding 300 to 500 inmates.

These buildings which became known as Houses of Industry were run under a tough no nonsense regime. In Suffolk twelve such establishments were created between 1756 and 1790. However significant areas of the county remained 'unincorporated', with individual parishes retaining responsibility for their own paupers. In fact surprisingly few existing parish workhouses in the county were affected by the appearance of the House of Industry. *(This can be seen in the coverage maps inside the front and rear cover pages).* Indeed more were being built. Parliamentary surveys carried out in 1803 and 1815 identify at least ten parishes that created workhouses in this period, though a similar number abandoned theirs[17]. Also the closure of the Loes & Wilford House of Industry at Melton in 1827, in readiness for its conversion into the county asylum, meant those parishes affected became responsible for their own poor. Some choosing the parish workhouse as a way forward.

The simultaneous existence of these two different systems led to an irregularity around the county. The sporadic coverage of the randomly created parish workhouse was in stark contrast to the blanket coverage of the hundredal-based Houses of Industry. Much of eastern Suffolk had followed the lead of the Colneis & Carlford Incorporation, which was the first to construct its House of Industry in 1756. Others who took the same road were Samford, and Mutford & Lothingland, both in 1763; Blything, and Wangford, 1764; Loes & Wilford, 1765, (disincorporated 1827); Bosmere & Claydon, 1766; Stow, 1778 and Cosford, 1780. The only hundred in East Suffolk which remained unincorporated was Plomesgate. Here parishes were still creating their own parish workhouses well into the nineteenth century. Tannington, Cransford and Iken created ones between 1803 and 1815[18], Parham only building theirs in 1824[19]. Three parishes encompassed by Hundredal incorporations chose to retain their independence. Hadleigh remained outside the Cosford 'union', Dunwich did not join Blything and Woodbridge stayed independent of Loes and Wilford.

A cluster of villages to the north of Stowmarket experienced a form of 'postcode' politics in the 1780s. Stowupland, Haughley and Wetherden now fell under the guise of the newly created Stow House of Industry. However their northern neighbours Bacton and Cotton had each established their own parish workhouses. Conversely their western neighbours Elmswell and Norton never created a parish workhouse, instead remaining outside the whole system of indoor relief until the birth of the Union Workhouse half a century later.

By the end of the eighteenth century there was a significant movement of the population from the country into towns[20]. The advent of the industrial revolution in creating mass employment, with better wages and conditions was instrumental in this migration The effect of this being the young and healthy moved into the towns, while the aged and infirm, in other words those most dependant on parish relief, were left in the villages. This created a significant imbalance between the rate-paying providers and the needy pauper. Life in the rural villages became desperate. In some cases parish officers actively encouraged parishioners to leave the villages in order to reduce the burden on the ratepayers. In the mid 1830s nearly 2,500 men, women and children were moved from Suffolk villages to manufacturing districts of Lancashire, Cheshire, and Yorkshire in just two years.

Following a national review into the whole subject of Poor Law, a report was published in 1834. In the report it was shown that in the period 1824-1831 the hundredal based Incorporations had been over 50 per cent more economical than the areas still covered by the parochial workhouse. The report used the Blything Hundred as an example of the advantages of these incorporations. It was shown for an annual charge of just £10, each parish within the catchment area received the services of a governor & matron, schoolmistress, superintendent, chaplain, clerk, house surgeon, and visiting guardians. Something individual parishes could never afford for themselves[21]. This review resulted in the creation of the New Poor Law Act of 1834[22], culminating with the introduction of the Union Workhouse, alias 'The Spike'. This effectively ended the reign of the parish workhouse as an ingredient of England's Poor Law.

=========

Farm boys gleaning the harvest

Chapter Two

ACQUISITION

Little Cornard

As explained it was the 'Old Poor Law' Acts of Elizabethan England in the second half of the sixteenth century which paved the way for the arrival of the Parish Workhouse. Suffolk was at the forefront of this reformation. When Henry Tooley died in 1551, some thirteen years before the 1564 Act; he laid the foundation in his will[23] for the setting up of a charity to provide for the poor of the borough of Ipswich. The Executors of his Will purchased an old disused Priory in the borough and converted it into Christ Church Hospital, part of which included a workhouse[24].

By 1577 Hadleigh had set aside one wing of its Guild Hall as a workhouse for children[25]. This had proved so successful the commissioners given the task of looking into the issue of poor relief prior to the 1601 Act, used it as an illustration[26]. Other Suffolk parishes which had their own workhouses in the sixteenth century included Eye (1593)[27], and Bury St Edmunds (1597)[28]. Gradually more of these establishments were appearing around the county.

Many influential parishioners and gentry saw the workhouse as a positive way of helping their able poor get back on their feet. In 1624 a legacy was left for *'a workin house'* in East Bergholt[29], though it is not certain if this one ever materialised. Equally it is not known if the letter transcribed in the foreword of this book produced the requested result. Dated 1622, it was written by one of the county's Justice of the Peace and sent to the overseer of the parish of Earl Stonham clearly instructing him to provide a workhouse for one of his parishioners[30].

Elsewhere an inventory dated 1664 provides proof of the existence of a workhouse in Aldeburgh[31]. In the same year one was built within Framlingham castle, though it would appear here demand was greater than anticipated. Within a few decades, when some older stone buildings with-in the grounds were pulled down in the 1680s, salvaged materials were used to extend the workhouse[32].

Knatchbulls' Act of 1722 did away with the hurdle a vestry previously encountered of applying to Parliament for authority to create a parish workhouse. Now all it had to do was to obtain a majority concensus of its parishioners, followed by the approval of the local Justice of the Peace. As a result more parishes saw the workhouse as a viable option for managing their poor. This signalled a proliferation of these cottage type workhouses. Vestry meetings were now occupied with the debate of the fors and againsts of this single issue. Parish officers would look to vestries with existing workhouses to see what could be learnt, with topics like costings and adaptations of premises high on the agenda. The accounts for the building of the workhouse at Lowestoft in 1739 include a disbursement of 6/6d paid to Robert Barker to cover his expenses for a trip to Southwold with Mr Gooding and Thomas Todd to view the workhouse there, presumably a fact finding mission[33].

Another element of the Knatchbull's Act was the encouragement of smaller parishes to merge to provide a joint workhouse. The most renowned instance of this happening in Suffolk was at Great Wratting, Great Thurlow, Chilborn and Barnardston. Here, as a result of the bequest of James Vernon[34], these parishes united to construct a combined workhouse to serve these four parishes. Boxford and Groton also applied to unite in 1765, though it would seem this never happened as records show they still had separate premises in the 1780s[35]. Groton possibly had a workhouse since 1616, which Lord of the Manor, John Winthrop had instructed his churchwardens and overseers to *'erect a house for the impotent poor on manorial waste by way from Wickerstreet to Castleins Heathe'*[36].

Parish workhouses sprang up all over the county. Of the five hundred plus parishes in Suffolk, one hundred and seventy nine have been identified as running a parish workhouse at one time or other. Initially it was the depressed areas around the old textile towns which saw the greatest numbers. Following the demise of the 'old draperies' in the late sixteenth - early seventeenth centuries, parishes around Lavenham, Sudbury and Haverhill, both large and small, found their numbers of unemployed on the increase. Later, towards the end of the eighteenth century it was the parishes to the north of the county along the Waveney valley, particularly around Eye and Bungay, which suffered the same fate, with the demise of the 'new draperies'. Rapidly expanding unemployment forced parish overseers and fellow officers to find ways of accommodating these queues of deserved needy.

The first issue which presented itself to the vestry of such parishes which decided to create a workhouse, was the procurement of the building. While the size of the demand on a particular parish was the crucial factor in the type of building sought, availability played a significant part in what was obtainable. In some cases existing buildings were adapted. Other parishes benefited from compassionate parishioners who gave properties to the parish, either as a lifetime gift, or by bequest on their death. Yet others made the decision to purchase buildings for conversion, while a few would decide to construct brand new purpose built properties. This variety of sources made for a variety of shapes and sizes, from those large Guild Halls which could accommodate anything up to 180 paupers, down to the smallest of parish cottages, such as at Somerleyton which had room for just three inmates[37].

Guild Halls were a legacy left over from the 'glory years' of textile wealth. Once the hub of social life, these substantial buildings were now left dormant, under the 'care' of the crown. Henry VIII had confiscated these buildings in 1546 as part of his dissolution programme[38]. Following his death in 1547 many parishes sought to repurchase these buildings and bring them back into social use. Some parishes, Hadleigh and Nayland in particular, converted theirs into a place of employment for their 'deserved poor'. It seems fitting that premises built on the wealth of an industry should ultimately provide accommodation for those hardest hit by the demise of that same industry.

The layout of these former social premises would have been ideal for the high numbers of unemployed in these towns. Surviving inventories for Hadleigh[39] suggest the main 'banqueting hall' on the ground floor with its fifty three spinning wheels would have been the main place of employment. Elsewhere on the ground floor, rooms were used for the associated weaving jobs like carding, combing and fulling. The kitchen, pantry and brewing rooms are all identified thus, The largest room on the first floor, over the workroom, accommodated eighteen bedsteads, which would, by inference, sleep up to seventy inmates. (It was commonplace for inmates to sleep up to four in a bed). Other rooms on this level held a total of twenty seven more beds, bringing the capacity of the house up to the 180 mark.

The size and layout of these premises provided potential advantages for parish officers and inmates alike, with separate committee rooms and governors quarters for the former, as well as the separation of sexes and ages for the latter. These premises were in effect a cross between a factory and a dormitory, with stress and frictions guaranteed when in excess of 100 inmates were required to live and work in a confined place. Other towns that utilised Guild Halls in this way included Lavenham[40], Nayland[41], Needham cum Barking[42], Palgrave[43] and Pakenham[44].

Of course not all parishes had access nor indeed needed such large premises. Many parishes owned 'town houses' or almshouses, which were used merely as accommodation for the poor and needy.

The majority of these pauper homes were more on the scale of semi detached or terraced rows of one up one down tenements. Constructed of wattle and daub walls, under a thatched roof, these were often in a poor structural condition with leaking roofs which let in the elements at will. With a room set aside for the governor, the inmates would be left with the minimum of space to carry out the daily rituals. In many cases as many as twenty five inmates would have had just three or four rooms in which to work, eat and sleep.

These properties would in reality have been little more than the 'hovels' Sir Edwin Chadwick lambasted in his report into the condition of labourer's cottages in 1834[45]. Always in need of repair, with broken windows, doors that did not shut properly, no fresh water, and little or no sanitation. They would have been damp, draughty residences reeking of the putrid stench, which lingered in the poorest streets of medieval England, prior to the introduction of underground sewerage systems in Victorian times. The conditions endured by inmates of these miniature hovels would have been of confined overcrowding, and an appalling environment unfit for human habitation.

While it is surely impossible to fully appreciate the life an inmate endured in these habitats of the seventeenth century, one of Suffolk's finest poets, George Crabbe, provided a vivid picture of the conditions which prevailed within the walls of a parish workhouse in his poem, of which an extract is included in the final chapter.

For a small rural parish with a population of between 100 and 200, a workhouse of two up two down arrangement would have been considered adequate to house the twenty to thirty inmates anticipated of such a population. The workhouse at Aldeburgh in 1664, which was claimed to hold up to fifteen inmates, contained *a little parler next the streete, a little ould room, a parler with a chamber above; a hall and hall chamber*[46]. The building used as a workhouse by the parish vestry at Cowling in 1817, (capacity 20), ran to a kitchen, shop, lamp room, with a large room set aside for George Parson, presumably the governor[47]. On this basis Somerleyton's recorded capacity of just three inmates implies either a building of one up one down arrangement, or an end terrace, as it is virtually certain a workhouse would not have been a mid terrace.

As mentioned some parishes gained from benevolent individuals. Present or former parishioners would bequest properties often into trusts set up for the benefit of a village or town. When Henry Tooley, *'the richest merchant in Ipswich'* died in 1551, he bequeathed most of his fortune to provide accommodation and relief for the poor of the town[48]. The Tooley Foundation was set up to administer his wishes. One of their first assignments was the acquisition of the former Priory of the Dominicans, alias the Black Friars, situated in what is now known as Foundation Street. This was purchased with monies raised by the selling of some of his properties in the borough. The building was then converted, with the refectory and main hall being adapted for use as a workhouse. Other parts of the building were used variously as an infirmary, gaol, and pauper's school[49].

Another of Suffolk's generous benefactors was James Vernon of Barnardston. When he died in 1747, he bequeathed his messuage Weathercock Farm to be used as a workhouse for the four parishes of Great Wratting, Great Thurlow, Chilborn & Barnardiston. He also endowed a yearly rent-charge of £10 out of other lands towards the cost of the management of the premises. He made further significant contributions towards providing workhouses in Hundon, Wickhambrook and Stradishall, again backed up with a trust fund for the churchwardens of Hundon to pay for a master of the workhouse at £10 per annum[50].

Elsewhere premises in Pound Street, Woodbridge, alias Theatre Street, were given by local merchant William Bearman for the benefit of the parish poor in 1668. This had become the workhouse by the early eighteenth century[51]. In 1713, £100 was provided by funds given by John Moor, for the purchase of a workhouse at Long Melford.[52] While the size of this initial building is not clear, it was extended in 1775 to bring its capacity up to 150, making it the largest workhouse in the county at the time. Surviving documents give detail of the builder's estimations for the renovation work. This involved the dismantling of the frame of another building in the town, fifty seven foot long and ten feet wide *'now standing at the back part of ye house late Mr Polley's and setting ye same up again in ye workhouse yard one end to join ye house'*[53].

Some parish officers chose renting as the means of acquiring premises. At Polstead in 1746, a group of principal inhabitants agreed to rent two tenements with outhouses, yards, gardens and orchards in the parish, currently being occupied by Thomas Ratcliff and John Humphrey, specifically *'for conversion into a workhouse'*. The rent for the property was set at £6 per annum for seven years. It is not clear if Thomas and John became eligible as inmates or if they were found alternative accommodation[54].

Many of these parish cottages would have been in a state of some disrepair; work would have been required to make them suitable for their new use. At Wingfield in 1757 a meeting of the churchwardens, overseers and other parishioners resolved to *'convert, alter and repair the town house into a workhouse …. for the purpose of employing and maintaining the poor of the parish'*. This included the pulling down the old chimney, cleaning the bricks and rebuilding a new chimney[55].

Renovations and extensions allowed some vestries to give old buildings a new lease of life, though the often significant outlay required was seen by others as too much a gamble, instead they took the decision to construct new premises, considering a purpose built property a more cost effective option in the long term. At Monks Eleigh when two cottages in Church Street were burnt down in 1766, a new workhouse was erected on the site[56]. In 1783 the vestry of Assington decided to construct a brand new workhouse. Surviving documents give full details of the costings with the final amount in the region of £230[57].

A meeting at Lowestoft in 1739 of the town's *'principal and other inhabitants called to consult upon measures for the benefit and relieve of the Poor,* concluded *'it highly neccessary and convenient to erect a workhouse for the support and maintenance of the poor.* It was decided to finance the venture through subscriptions. A total sum of £140 was achieved by loans of £10 lots[58]. Financing these projects came from a variety of sources, Brandon used some of the £1,600 obtained through a scheme set up by one of its former residents William Brewster, a malster and quaker; to build a two-storey chalk workhouse, situated in Church End, with a house for the governor built adjacent to it[59].

One of the final parishes to construct a workhouse in the county was Parham. On 4th December 1822 a loan of £300 was arranged to fund the erection of a workhouse on North Green. In 1835 following the formation of the Plomesgate Union, this workhouse was used as a temporary refuge for the aged poor from Framlingham workhouse until a new Union building was constructed in Wickham Market some two years later[60].

It would seem Kettleburgh was the final parish in the county, if not country, to choose to venture down the road of the parish workhouse. They had originally been swallowed up by the Loes & Wilford Incorporation in 1765. However this establishment was unincorporated in 1827, with the county magistrates purchasing the former House of Industry building, situated at Melton, for the county's first Asylum. The parishes affected by this move suddenly found themselves singularly responsible for the care of their poor. The reaction of the Kettleburgh vestry was to construct a workhouse on charity lands in the village[61].

It is clear that over the two hundred or so years of the existence of these establishments, some parishes used more than one building as a workhouse, be it at different times. Sometimes there was a gap in between when the parish reverted to maintaining their poor solely through out-relief. The new house built in Assington, as mentioned above, would seem to have been a replacement for the one sited in 'part of the blacksmith shop' in 1760[62]. The parish officers deciding a new one was a more practical investment. Equally a reference to a workhouse in New Street, Woodbridge[63] offers an alternative location to the property bequeathed by William Bearman in Theatre Street.

The most obvious reason for more than one building being utilised as a workhouse, would be the condition of these premises.

This in itself made for a limited lifespan. Wattle and daub walls and straw thatched roofs were prone to succumb to the vagaries of the inclement British weather. The plastered walls would crumble and fall off. Straw used on the thatched roofs would not have had the lifespan of the superior but costly Norfolk reed. Being a more brittle product it would have required constant repair. While this ensured regular work for local builders, there would inevitably come a time when even these hovel-like buildings would become beyond repair.

When new premises were sought, many considered the best location was on the outskirts of the parish. This was due largely to the stench, disease, and virus which accompanied these primitive establishments. Equally the amount of trouble and violence which often seemed an endemic part of the parish workhouse was something most of society found in the least obnoxious, in the extreme, unbearable. The workhouse at Saxmundham was an example of the ideal location, situated on the western extreme of the township, well outside the parish boundary line of the time[64]. When the Boxted vestry chose to construct a new property in 1791, they identified a piece of land *'on the waste'*. As this land belonged to the Lord of the Manor, his consent had to first be obtained[65]. Friston's parish workhouse was situated on the Moor[66] and Parham decided to build theirs on vacant grounds on North Green, again well away from the hub of the village[67].

However to forgive the retort, beggars could not be choosers, many parish officers had to be far more realistic when it came to acquiring premises. Where town or alms-houses were utilised, these were often in the centre of the parish. At Dennington, when the vestry committee sought suitable premises for a workhouse, they turned to a dwelling situated on the south side of the crossroads within walking distance of its church. Known as Goldings and Sowgates, it had originally been conveyed to parish trustees in 1606 by Rev. Edward Green, for the relief of the poor[68]. Other instances of workhouses being in the heart of the village include Monks Eleigh where it was situated in Church Street close to the village green[69]. Likewise the one at Stonham Aspall sat beside the church[70].

Parish vestries must have been bedazzled by the number of Acts which appeared in the sixteenth and early seventeenth centuries relating to workhouses. The local parish dignitaries who made up these Vestry committees would have spent many hours debating the implications of this provocative and revolutionary new system of dealing with poor law. Some saw these new laws as a window of opportunity in their efforts to control the mounting cost of providing out relief for the poor. Others treated them with trepidation, envisaging the workhouse would become a liability without getting to the real issue of providing regular employment for the deserved poor.

As mentioned earlier, the location and costings of a workhouse was a contentious issue. An example of this happened at a public meeting held in the parish church at Barking on Wednesday 23rd August 1727. Top of the agenda was the implications of a resolution made at a previous meeting held on 27th June. The decision had been taken to convert the almshouses at Needham for the use of a workhouse to serve the two parishes. A steering committee, made up of sixteen persons from the two villages had been delegated to manage the project. However following much heated debate, the outcome of this second meeting was to overturn the initial decision. Instead it was agreed to convert the Guild Hall at Barking, currently being used as a Free School. As this building had originally been gifted to the parish by Sir Frances Theobald, the consent of the feoffees of his trust had to be obtained.

The original steering committee was then entrusted with the responsibility of all matters relating to the conversion and equipping of the workhouse. This included securing the finances required, with the rate payers of the parish picking up any shortfall. It was further agreed any loans secured for the project were to be repaid quarterly at an interest rate of 10d in the pound, until repaid in full. A subsequent statement of accounts show the final figure required was £210 12s 7½d. This amount was initially achieved by loans of £100 from Mrs Ruffells; £60 from Mr Parker and £8 14s 0d from Thomas Chenery. With £41 18s 7½d being received from the overseer's accounts, the final amount levied on the ratepayers was £20 16s 2d, equating to just 10% of the original cost[71].

When Brandon built their house in 1728, it was initially funded by a loan from William Brewster's charity. The parish accounts for 1738 reveal the final figure for the cost of the workhouse was £200 6s 1d, with a further £35 15s 5½d spent on furnishing the workhouse. The same accounts then show how the money was raised in order for the loan to be repaid. The sum of £158 4s 6d was received from various individuals with £10 being the norm. This money was then invested to obtain sufficient interest to meet this short-fall[72].

The same Brandon accounts give a breakdown of the construction costs for their workhouse. Here we learn the building was constructed with 14,000 white bricks and 12,000 'lining' bricks at a cost of 20/- and 18/- per thousand respectively. The 9,600 tiles required for the roof cost £9 12s 0d. Timber deals came in various denominations: 'very broad', 'thick', 'splits' and 'halves'.

Sixty eight loads of chalk @ £3 19s 4d; forty four chaldrons and thirty four bushel of quick lime @ £22 8s 6d; thirty bushel of hair @ £1 2s 6d; eighteen bunches of heart laths @ 2/9d each, and thirty one bunches of sap laths which cost 18d each, would have been used to create the wattle and daub used in the construction of the wall. Other items included a doorpost and lintel at 5/11d, and two mantle pieces which cost £1 3s 0d. There is one all-inclusive entry of *nails, joints locks etc £4 10s 10d.* all of which contributing to the overall total of £200 6s 1d.

For a comparison between the costs of building a new workhouse against that of converting existing premises, the Brandon construction cost of £200 6s 1d, be it in 1728, can be set against the costs incurred by Wingfield vestry in 1757. The conversion and repair of their workhouse cost just £31 3s 11d. Here an estimate for work put forward by Thomas Card of Stradbroke, included 3,000 delivered bricks £4 17s 6d, and five chaldron of lime £3 6s 8d, while 1,500 plain tile and twenty roof tiles cost £2 8s 4d. Further entries include: *'for pouling down the old stayrs and putting up the new* and *finding all materials 14/-'.* To pull down the old chimney, clean the bricks, and build a new chimney with two fire hearths, together with '*an oven and convayancy for hanging a copper*' cost another £5 5s 0d. For making good the floor where the chimney and stays come down 17/6d[73].

The Brandon vestry found themselves confronted with a legal situation in 1778. The ownership of the workhouse was put in question as a result of insufficient feoffees being available to run the parish. This meant the possession of the workhouse reverted back into the hands of Rowland Holt, esq. The Lord of the Manor at the time. Only when sufficient new persons had been sworn in did the ownership of the workhouse be released to the parish *"by the hands of his steward to certain Feoffees at this time"*[74].

Another instance of trustees falling foul of workhouse laws happened in 1790 at St Matthews, Ipswich. When the original deed for the creation of the workhouse was drawn up, it stipulated all trustees were to live within the boundaries of the parish. This ruling was picked up in 1790 by one of the vestry when the deed was inspected on another matter. The outcome being two trustees Reverand Mr Layton and Mr William Kindell, neither of whom lived in the parish were declared 'improper trustees' and removed from their position. Their replacements were Mr Joseph Flundell & Mr Samuel Atkinson[75].

========

Chapter Three

EQUIPMENT and MAINTENANCE

Wetheringsett

Once a vestry had acquired its premises and carried out any conversion work, the next priority was to source the equipment required to run the workhouse. This would include basic furnishings like beds and linen, tables, chairs and storage cupboards. Cooking equipment such as saucepans, pans, various fire irons, trenchers, kettles, knives and forks were needed, as well as incidental items like baskets, linen lines, clothes horses, coppers and brooms. Other items necessary included those required to carry out whatever type of employment was to be undertaken in the workhouse. Such items may include spinning wheels, garden tools, mash tubs, keelers, and troughs

The methods of obtaining stock were as wide and varied as sourcing the premises. As explained the responsibility for this fell into the hands of the overseer. Along with his vestry committee he would identify, then acquire the basic essentials required from whatever source he could. At Brandon in 1737 we learn the overseers bought £35 15s 5½d worth of furniture to stock their workhouse. This included two beds from John Docken for £3 0s 0d; four beds were obtained from Thomas Mather together with blankets and rugs which amounted to a total cost of £6 10s 0d; with a further two beds, bedsteads and bedding bought from elsewhere for £3 12s 6d. These possibly came from Mildenhall Fair for there is a payment of 3/6d made for the *carriage of goods from Milden fair.* This quantity of beds would have proved sufficient for the capacity of twenty one as given in the 1776 Poor Law Survey, based on the typical ratio of one bed per four inmates[76].

Other items brought into the Brandon house included three wheels, with reel and carriage at 8/6d; and nine spinning wheels costing 13/6d which were obviously for the employment of the inmates. Equally a mash tub and two killers at 17/- would be equipment used in the brewing process, another area of potential employment for the inmates. A lot of workhouses had rooms set aside for making ale, the primary beverage for everyday consumption. Whilst a few inventories included tea in their listings, this would have been a relatively exclusive and expensive item, probably for the governor or parish officers when visiting. Water was definitely not of a quality suitable for drinking. Ale was stored in hogsheads, a type of barrel capable of holding 48 gallon of ale, with a half hogshead used in the smaller establishments. Some other incidentals at Brandon include: a pair of bellows and other items at 6/9d, a coal grate for the kitchen at £1 2s 0d, while *'nineteen pieces of pewter'* at 14/3d would have been items such as jugs and drinking vessels for the inmates.

At Hadleigh £5 left by John Freeman in 1592 was spent on bedding for the workhouse[77]. Three years later in 1595 the overseer recorded he had bought thirteen spinning wheels for the thirty paupers who were employed in spinning yarn for sale to the Norfolk weavers[78]. The overseer of Sudbourne's accounts show that in April 1817 he bought a pair of bedsteads for 15/-. About a month later he bought four wooden dishes and six plates for the costly sum of 3/-. Either the plates were best china, which is doubtful, or the bed very good value[79].

Obviously different parishes had differing budgets at their disposal. It would seem a parish workhouse with a capacity of between thirty and fifty inmates could be kitted out in the mid eighteenth century for something in the region of £50. A memorandum written by overseer John Barber in 1747 values '*all the furniture in Metfield workhouse and elsewhere belonging to the parish*' at £60 14s 10d[80].

While it would be the more wealthy and affluent members of the community who were involved in the purchasing of the premises, virtually anyone in the parish could contribute to the goods and chattels required inside the workhouse. One individual might offer a couple of chairs, another would provide some cutlery. When a new governor took over the running of a workhouse they would often bring equipment with them. According to the overseer's accounts, when Bridget Stamford became governor at St Mary at the Elm's, Ipswich in 1762 she brought several 'goods and chattels' including a bed, two chairs, a table, two spinning wheels and several kitchen utensils[81].

Once the premises were kitted out, one of the responsibilities of the parish overseer was to maintain good stock control. It was to this end regular inventories were carried out, normally on an annual basis or at the time of a change of governor. Usually the parish overseer himself would carry out this stock-take, but there were occasions when the job was delegated to other parish officials. As there was no overall ruling on how these stock-takes were to be carried out or indeed recorded, the style and content of surviving inventories can vary enormously. No doubt the quality and quantity of detail mirrored the skills level of the officers designated to carry out the stock-take. Some, like the one for Clare, included all equipment whether usable or in obvious disrepair[82], while others, like that at Cratfield[83] were no more than a list of items, as basic as the incumbents writing skills, no doubt the two matters being linked. Only a few surviving inventories include individual costing, suggesting the worth lay with the object rather than any transient value.

The content of these inventories provide us with a valuable insight into various aspects of life at this period of time. Firstly their very existence provides proof of the existence of a particular establishment. The information within shows the quantity, (and often quality) of the goods and chattels which furnished the workhouse. They demonstrate the importance of commodities of the period, candles and kettles; and antiquities such as trenchers (a wooden plate) or a hogshead used for storing ale. By including items even when 'broken' or 'badly worn' they demonstrate the prudence and astuteness of those whose job it was to balance the books.

Inventories can hold clues to the type of work carried out in an establishment. While the spinning wheel is the constant piece of equipment throughout, items like gardening tools in the Assington workhouse and calf pens and pig trough at Clare suggest livestock was being reared, probably for the pot. Another area of employment in the workhouse was the brewing room. Coppers, coolers, keelers, mash tubs, and wort skips were all used in the fermenting process.

Furthermore these inventories highlight the literary capabilities of these 'local dignitaries' who were responsible for their compilation. The grammar and spelling would demonstrate the level of education of those churchwardens & overseers who compiled these inventories. For this reason it is necessary to appreciate much of the written word of the period was spelt as heard; hence in order to gain an accurate translation of any document of the period, knowledge of the local tongue is of considerable value. The Suffolk dialect tends to drop the ends off words, and to roll its Rs hence *pudding* becomes *pudn; bed* becomes *bead or baird,* chair becomes *cheair* etc. etc .

Two such inventories have been selected from different parts of the county for a closer analysis of their content. They have been translated into modern English to give clarity to the various aspects. The first is for the workhouse in Wetheringsett, a parish situated in the central northern part of the county, known as High Suffolk. It enjoyed a population in the region of 300 parishioners at the time of the inventory.

The second inventory is of the furnishings etc in the Haverhill workhouse. Situated in the southwestern corner of the county, Haverhill at the time of the inventory had a population of 1,216. However as the 1776 survey of parish workhouses shows a capacity for this parish's establishment of just forty inmates, the inventory count of thirty seven beds (*implying a figure more in the region of 100 to 120 paupers*), suggest either some significant extension had been undertaken or a different building was being used. Following the advent of the 1834 Poor Law Act, an even greater makeover of this workhouse took place, in order to accommodate up to 280 inmates from the whole of the Risbridge Union.

The first, taken from: *Wetheringsett Churchwardens Accounts 1730-1743*[84];

An Inventory of the goods in the workhouse, October the 6th 1740; in the possession of Thomas Skipper.

4 beds & 1 bed belonging to goody Kerry, eight Sheets, two blankets three Coverlets & one Coverlet of goody Kerry's, four bolsters, two pillows, five bedsteads, eleven chairs, seven broad trenchers, five spoons, five dishes, one pudding spoon, one wooden dish, one La Cup, one earthern dish, one pudding pan, 29 mugs, one large pound tub, two pails, two iron pots, one pair of pothakes, two warming pans, two press cupboards, one wash basket, one settle, [illegible], one La hutch, four Tables, one pair cob irons, pair fire Shovel & Tongs, one hale, one pair bellows, four shelves, one sto? lock on ye dairy door, one stock lock on ye kitchen door, one dresser, one copper as it hang, one wort sieve, two skillets, four killers.

(Items) lent of goody Batty: one of ye two ale Stools, one peel, two flour sieves, one beer vessel, one old latch, ye beer vessel to be cut, two killers, one frying pan, four wheels, one reel & 2 pair bleeds, 1 tool

October 6th 1741

six wooden bottom chairs, four pottage dishes, a dozen earthern half penny plates, two red earth dishes, two towels, four pudding bags, a course sieve, a pail, a ladle,

April 20th 1742

Two pair sheets, a wash basket, & a large hand, basket, a coal grate, three small iron bars & sifter.

....

31

And secondly taken from: *Haverhill Parish Records. Inventory of Furniture 1813 & 1815[85];*

1813}/
Feb 1ˢᵗ } Jnventory of the Furniture Etc of / the Parish House as taken by the/ Revᵈ Fraˢ Merewether Vicar and / Mr James Symonds Churchwarden / No 1 Committee Room / Writing Desk / 2 Tables, gave to Chaˢ Cornell / 6 Elbow wooden Chairs / 6 Plain Dᵒ / 1 Stove & set of Fire Jrons / 1 Coal Scuttle / 1 Large Arm Chair.
　　　　No 2 Committee Room Closets.
41 pair of Shoes / 3 parts of pieces of Calico / A Tub with Sugar / 24 Bricks of Soap / 6 lbs of Candles / 4 Packetts of Bills etc.
　　　　Committee Room Garretts.
1ˢᵗ: 34 Cheeses / 2ⁿᵈ: The furniture of Nathᵉˡ Webbs.
　　　　governors Sleeping Room.
Chest of Drawers / 4 Bedsteads.
　　　　Widows Sleeping Room.
No 1. Bed and Bedstead / No 2. Dᵒ Dᵒ & Bedding {Brid widow / No 3. Dᵒ Dᵒ Dᵒ. {wid Webbs) / No 4. Dᵒ Dᵒ Dᵒ {wid Fuller.
　　　　No 6 Sleeping Room.
No 1 Bed Bedstead & Bedding {wid Farr. / No 2. Dᵒ Dᵒ Dᵒ {Parish / No 3. Dᵒ Dᵒ Dᵒ { Rug in Kiddys / No 4. Dᵒ Dᵒ Dᵒ {Wm Webbs / Cribb and Bedding {Dᵒ.
　　　　No 7. Sleeping Room.
No 1 Bed bedstead & Bedding {R.P. Jⁿᵒ Spall / No 2. Dᵒ Dᵒ Dᵒ {Parish / No 3. Dᵒ Dᵒ Dᵒ { Dᵒ / No 4. Dᵒ Dᵒ Dᵒ {. R.P. Mary Whiff / No 5. Dᵒ Dᵒ Dᵒ {Parish / No 6. Dᵒ Dᵒ Dᵒ { Dᵒ / The Table late Antony Walters
　　　　No 8. Sleeping Room
2 Beds, Bedsteads & Bedding
　　　　No 9. Sleeping Room
No 1. Bed, Bedstead & Bedding {Parish / No 2. Dᵒ Dᵒ Dᵒ { Parish / No 3. Dᵒ Dᵒ Dᵒ { R.P. /
　　　　Kitchen
3 dozn tin plates / [illeg.] 2 Large pewter dishes / A Boiler and 2 Coppers / A Frying Pan / 3 earthen pots, & 6 earthen dishes
　　　　Skullery
16 Trenchers / 1 Wash hand bason / A Tea Kettle
　　　　Dining Room

A Beam & pair of Scales / 4 /2 and In hundred weights / A sack barrow / 4 dining Boards, and / 8 Stools, & sundry trussels / A Grate / A Clothes Horse / A Ladder / 3 Clothes Basketts.

Wash House

4 Wart Tubs / Brewing Copper / Washing Copper / Mash Tub / 5 Wash keilers / 3 Washing Stools / Grindstone and frame / Cooler and Water trough.

No 1 Cellar.

5 Hogshead casks / 2 Pork Tubs / 11 Brush brooms/ ~~1 small cask~~ C Cornell / 3 Ale Stools

No 2 Cellar

2 Ash Casks / A Bushel Measure / 1 half D^o / 2 pecks and ¼ of a peck.

No 3 Cellar/

1 Cask / 1 Old Tub

Weaving Shop/

2 Looms compleat / 2 D^o Old / 1 D^o &c of Nathaniel Wells / 1 Wire Sieve

No 1 Mens Sleeping Room

7 Beds, Bedding and Bedsteads

No 2 Womans Sleeping Room

No 1 Bed, Bedstead, & Bedding {widow Backlan / No 2 D^o & Blankett (Rash's) the rest Parish / No 3 D^o Bedstead & Bedding (parish / A Chair and Table / No 4 Bed Bedstead & Bedding {Do / No 5 D^o D^o D^o Lettices

Mens Garrett

No 1 Bed, Bedstead & Bedding {Turners) / No 2 D^o D^o D^o {J^{no} Darking).

Womans Garrett.

No 1 Bed, Bedstead, & Bedding / (R.P.) part (R Barit) & Chair / No 2 Bed Bedstead & Bedding {W Nunn) / No 3 D^o D^o D^o {R Beavis / No 4 D^o D^o D^o {Parish / No 5 D^o D^o D^o {D^o

Spinning Room

7 Spinning Wheels, frames &c

Widows Keeping Room

A Table / 3 Old Chairs

governors Keeping Room No 1

~~A Corner Cubboard~~ \C Cornell/ & (Square / Cannister & Tea Caddy / 2 Brass Candlesticks / 3 Iron Candlesticks / Pair of Snuffers & Stand / Box Jron rest /

governors Keeping Room No 2

~~A Clock~~ C Cornell / Stove & fire irons & fender / Cheese Clock, & bread Knife / A Large Deal Table / A Round Table (Eliz^h Baileys.

Pantry
3 Cubboards / 30 breakfast Tins / 1 Hutch. / 1 Writing Table /
Chest of Drawers (C Sparrow / 1 9 gallon Cask / 1 Treakle D° / 1
Salt Tub / 1 Flour D° / A Joint Stool / A small beam, & Scales /
14lb bloom weights / A pair of Steps / A Tin Cann (Old) / 1 doz of
Wooden Spoons / A Tin Lamp.

. . . .

The opening paragraph of the Wetheringsett inventory, by identifying the property in the workhouse as being in the 'possession of' Thomas Skipper suggest this workhouse was being 'farmed out' to him. Furthermore it would appear Goody Kerry had brought her own bed and bed linen with her, though it is not clear if she was an inmate or an employee, possibly the cook. The phrase 'goody' merely means a single woman of some age, either spinster or widowed. There is the usual mixture of cooking and fireside aids: pudding dishes, keelers, skillets, a pair of cobiron, fire shovel and tongs, bellows. Ale Stools and beer vessels illustrate brewing was carried out on the premises.

The count of five beds suggest a capacity in the region of twenty inmates, which roughly compares with the 1776 survey figure of twenty five. Obviously numbers would vary from one season to another, and year to year. However the small amount of crockery does suggest the house was nowhere near capacity.

Moving onto the second inventory, for Haverhill, we learn it was the local vicar, the Reverend Merewether, and churchwarden Mr Symonds who carried out the stock-take. These would certainly have been on the parish vestry. The identity of two committee rooms coupled with the large number of bedrooms demonstrate the size of this workhouse, which would have been on the scale of a Guild Hall. While there is ample furnishings in the committee rooms including elbow chairs, there is an obvious lack of equipment elsewhere, especially in the kitchen and bedrooms. In fact there would seem to be a general lack of organisation with ladders and clothes horses being stored in the dining room.

There are plenty of items for brewing and storing ale. Five hogsheads would provide sufficient capacity for 200 gallons of ale, although it is very likely at least one of them would have been used for wines for the committee members. It is interesting that the candles are measured by weight rather than number. The inclusion of separate spinning and weaving rooms further demonstrates the size of the premises, though again there is a definite lack of equipment other than the basics.

These two inventories show the contrasting type of premises used as parish workhouses. While a two up two down labourer's cottage would have adequately served small rural parishes, the larger towns and boroughs would have required something on the scale of the Guild Halls to accommodate the number of inmates. They also demonstrate how these differing enterprises were run in differing ways. The smaller affair would carry out general working practices in the same rooms as inmate had their meals, with a single room set aside for the governor himself. However the larger premises would have the benefit of a far greater selection of rooms for the committee and the governor, as well as having the facilities for separation of sexes and age groups. It can be seen this did not necessarily make for a more organised house.

. . . .

Having acquired the premises and equipment necessary to function, there would have been an ongoing need for maintenance of both. The very nature of the buildings, while sound in their framework, meant they were always in need of repair. Often constructed of former ships timbers which would have already stood the test of a century or two, especially in the case of the Guild Halls and their like. These building would actually move with the wind, something which allowed them to withstand far greater forces than solid buildings of more recent times. However, as referred to earlier, the wattle and daub which was used as infill, and the straw thatched roofs, were both far less durable materials, and susceptible to the constant changes in the British climate. The baking hot sun in summer contrasting with frost and rain in winter would ensure regular work for the local builders. The accounts for the workhouse at Saxmundham show how varied maintenance costs could be. During the period 1794 to 1834, yearly amounts of anything between 12/9d up to £31 10s 0d were made for *'repairs or alterations of the workhouse*[86]. Entries in the Helmingham churchwarden's accounts in 1753 include 10/- for someone *fetching the clay and carrying it to the workhouse*, and 1/6d for *straw to make the clay*, with a further 10/- paid for *daubing all the workhouse*[87]. This may well have been for a new shell of rendering, to keep it in good repair.

At Wetheringsett in November 1732, the churchwardens made a payment of 13/- to an unnamed carrier *"for carriage of 350 bricks to the town house, ... fetching a load of sand and carrying two hundred and 9 lb? of bricks and 6 bushelll of lime.* Other maintenance entries in this book include the sum of 12/6d paid for 'five Rodd of ditching at the workhouse' in November 1733, then in October 1740 3/- was paid for carrying 3 trees from Tho Vinsons to the workhouse[88]. The ditching would have been a regular requirement in a rural parish; this would have been the means by which liquid waste was channelled from the house. In the towns open gullies were routed along the streets for the same purpose.

The various accounts of the parish churchwardens and overseers are literally littered with entries relating to the day-to-day costs of workhouse maintenance. At Redlingfield the churchwarden made half yearly payments of 3/- to the local chimney-sweep, with further monthly payments to an unnamed carrier for 'coals to the house'[89]. The Orford accounts show Daniel Simson being paid 2/- 'by order of the maide' for cleaning the well at the workhouse. Then on 8th June 1764 he was paid 3/6 for straw and carting to the workhouse, obviously the local odd job man.

Bearing in mind most properties in the eighteenth century had basic earth floors, this straw may have been used for littering the floors[90]. Littering was widely used both as bedding and a means of sanitation. Akin to what is now reserved for animal care of such as horses and cows.

Another type of bill was recorded at Wetheringsett in 1738 where the overseer *paid ye Constables Rate for the Workhouse 1d.*[91] This would have been payment for work carried out in relation to implementing the poor law, such as the incident which happened at Stoke by Nayland in December 1799. Here the constable was ordered to remove William Stow, his wife and two children from their own home to the workhouse, obviously against their will[92].

Most of the above costs were variable running costs, being affected by weather, time of year or number of inmates. However there were also fixed costs which arose no matter what. Parish workhouses were as liable for property taxes as any other premises. It is surviving land tax records for the workhouses at St Margarets in 1721[93] and St Matthews in 1729[94], which provide the earliest identified references of individual parish workhouses in Ipswich. Significantly these were the two largest parishes in the borough. In 1721 the property in St Margaret's had a rateable value of £10, with a rate charge of 1/6d, while in 1771 St Matthews was given a rateable value of £5, with a quarterly charge of 5/- being imposed[95]. One of their neighbours, St Lawrence, one of the smaller parishes in the borough both in population and area, was charged just 12/- for the whole year some twenty years later in 1799[96].

There are instances of parish officers appealing against the charges. When Walsham le Willows workhouse was assessed in 1785, a rent charge of 2/4d was issued. Following a successful appeal by the overseer, this was halved to 1/2d[97]. The Orford Chamberlain's accounts show annual payments between 1755 and 1767 of £2 for rent for the workhouse due on either Michaelmas Day being 29th September or St Stephens Day, 26th December[98]. Most transactions of this nature were carried out at one of the four quarter days, Lady Day, Midsummer Day, Michaelmas Day or Christmas Day. Another fixed cost particularly in the larger towns and boroughs was that of water rentals. Ipswich had its own water supply from the early seventeenth century. By 1802 charges in St Lawrence Ipswich were 5/6d a quarter, but St Helens vestry had to find 7/6d. for the same period[99].

The most common form of financing workhouse costs was through a poor rate charge, as had been directed by the 1601 Act of Parliament. Most vestries would initially try to source other methods in order to lessen the burden on the parish purse. We learn from the Brandon town book, the principal inhabitants of the town held a public meeting on 20th April 1778 at 'The Ram Inn', home of Henry

Taylor. One of the items on the agenda was the funding of necessary repairs to the workhouse. The outcome being the Rev. Thomas Ball, John Brewster, and James Denton each lent £100. For this they received 5 per cent interest on their loans. The Brandon vestry was obviously financially astute, for within the detail of the rules governing the monthly meetings of the workhouse committee, it was decreed that any person *"absenting or shall not appear at any meeting by seven of ye clock shall forfeit one shilling, and that every person, who shall make ye least motion[sic] for spending more than one shilling at a meeting shall forfeit one shilling. The forfeitures, when they amount to ten shillings to be spent as ye Society shall direct"*[100].

The structure of these properties would have made these premises very vulnerable to fire, be it by accident or deliberate. Following the Great Fire of London in 1666, fire insurance companies such as the Sun and Royal Exchange were developed whereby owners of properties could insure against such eventualities. Just about any type of building could be covered, so it is of no surprise vestries, many of whom were business people themselves choose to insure workhouses. In 1793 the Worlingworth vestry took out an insurance policy with Sun Fire Insurance for their workhouse. The policy was for £300 worth of cover and cost 15/- with a stamp duty of 4/6d. The cost and cover remained the same until at least 1808, though by then the stamp duty had risen to 7/6. Some things never change. The policy identifies the property as being of plaster, clay and thatch construction[101]. Other parishes which took out insurance cover included Hepworth[102] and Stoke by Clare[103] in 1795 and Groton in 1803[104].

Whether the Occold vestry chose to insure or not is unknown. They would have certainly been glad if them had in 1800, when their property was set alight by arsonists. An advertisement placed in the Ipswich journal on 8th March gave detail of a £50 reward for any person giving information 'that shall discover the offender'. A footnote mentioned the reward together with a full pardon would be given should any accomplice come forward with information[105].

===========

Chapter Four

MANAGEMENT STRUCTURE

Brandon

The management structure of these parish workhouses was reasonably simple. The principal figure was the overseer of the poor. Established by the Poor Law Act of 1597, the office of overseer was chosen from the parish vestry and normally ran for a year. The vestry itself was made up of rate-payers and land owners within the parish. The key role of the overseer was to manage the *'deserved poor'*, including the provision of the means for their employment. The workhouse being an important component within this agenda. Once a workhouse had been acquired, the officers would seek out a 'manager' to specifically take charge of the day to day running of the workhouse. The terminology for this position could vary from governor, governess, master or matron. *(for continuity hereafter this position will be referred to as governor).*

Most governors would be employed on a contractual basis, usually for a period of between one and five years. Initially the overseer retained overall control of the running of the workhouse. However following Knatchbull's Act of 1722[106], and the introduction of 'farming out', many governors were contracted to take responsibility for the whole concept of the workhouse, including the financing and maintenance of inmates and employment.

Bearing in mind the overall intention was to create a place of temporary residence, one which acted more as a deterrent than a hotel, therefore a prime requirement when seeking a new governor was for someone of strong uncompromising character. A person of good standing with strong religious background was foremost on the list. Management skills were welcome, inexperience frown upon. Advertisements placed in local newspapers, in particular the Ipswich Journal; highlight the criteria looked for by the various vestries. At Saxmundham in 1818 an advert placed in this newspaper sought a man and his wife to superintend the workhouse pointing out *'that any person not qualified for the job need not apply*[107].

Parishes would invariably state a minimum age for potential candidates. When St Margaret's Ipswich advertised for a governor and governess in 1819, they invited applicants without a family, and under the age of forty five. The overseers of Woodbridge specified the age group targeted as not less than thirty years nor more than fifty. At Wilby in 1803 a woman aged between forty and fifty was sought to be employed as governess of the poor, *'good wages were to be given'*. However some parishes were less specific. When the Benhall overseers required a governor they merely stated that applicants should be *'already accustomed'* to such a position.

The importance religion played in every day life in England, was mirrored by the requirement of virtually any candidate to be of Church of England faith. In 1813 at Haverhill they required a married man of the 'Established Church', with strong testimonials of his character and fitness for the situation. Furthermore it was claimed 'indispensable' that he should possess knowledge of the sack industry, emphasising the importance of the 'production' side of the establishment. Likewise when Bury St Edmunds advertised in February 1782 for a couple for their workhouse, it was stipulated the man should be well acquainted with either the wool trade or a keeper of a turnpike gate[108]. In 1765 the overseers at Debenham advertised for *'A sober man and woman capable of taking on the government of the Workhouse including the understanding of spinning of wool*[109]. Interested persons were to forward a character 'reference' of their honesty and abilities to the churchwardens and overseers of the parish.

As in all walks of life, the vestries did not always get what they wanted. On the same page of the Ipswich Journal as the Bury advertisement, the Hadleigh churchwardens and overseers also invited applications for a man and his wife to undertake the care and management of their workhouse poor. However when they drew up an agreement with Robert Tiler just four weeks later on 2nd April, there is no mention of a wife at all[110].

Various methods of remunerations were used by different vestries. While some, like those at St Margaret's Ipswich in 1755, paid their governor a weekly wage, here 1 shilling a week[111]; others preferred a contractual arrangement, normally drawn up for periods of between one and five years. Records for East Bergholt suggest the post was an annual one with four different governors identified there between 1734 and 1739[112]. An advert placed in the Ipswich Journal by Framsden vestry in 1817 required a person *'desirous of taking the poor of the workhouse'* for a period of three years. At Boxford on 30th March 1764, the Churchwardens of the parish took on William Ide, a yeoman of Nayland, for three years. For this he was to receive £114 1s 10d, which works out at approximately £38 per annum. When John Bear of Groton took over the same workhouse in 1785 his salary for the next five years was set at £46 per annum[113].

Governor's wages could vary enormously. As early as 1599 John Allen received the seemingly princely sum of £20 per annum for agreeing to 'operate the workhouse' at Hadleigh[114]. However not all governors received this sort of income. In 1794 the overseers of Saxmundham paid their new governor just 5 guineas per annum. Even in 1818 the regular wage for the new governor here was set at just £10 per annum, though in his first year he received £20[115]. Had the premises become rundown as a result of a lack of incentive provided by the meagre income for the previous master? If so, it would appear the establishment was promptly turned around. When Henry Stuart published his report in 1834 on poor relief in East

Anglia he identified Saxmundham along with Framlingham, as being 'most comfortable places' meaning they were too comfortable for the intended purpose[116].

Another method of payment saw governors paid according to the number of inmates. At East Bergholt in 1758 the governor received payments of between 1/- and 1/3 a week per inmate. It would appear any additional expenditure had to be authorised by the overseer, for he later requested '*10/- expences to buy goods for the workhouse*'. When Joseph Turner took over as the new governor he was allowed an extra guinea 'for cleaning the workhouse'[117].

As mentioned one of the rudiments of Knatchbull's Act in 1722 was the option for parishes to 'farm out' elements of their poor law management. This allowed parish overseers to draw up contracts with individuals to assume responsibility for the whole concept of the workhouse. For an agreed lump sum the governor would take over the financing & management of the workhouse and inmates as well as the implementation of any employment carried out within the premises. The contract agreed between the parish vestry of Pakenham and Robert Buxton, a worster weaver from Walsham, in October 1791 illustrate how this would work. Robert was to receive the seemingly princely sum of £200 to be paid over twelve monthly instalments[118]

However from this he had to pay all bills relating to the day to day management of the workhouse. This was to include providing '*good and sufficient clothes and lodgings, & diet*' as detailed by the overseers. Other bills which he had to cover included any charges relating to the sickness or deaths of inmates, as well as repair or replacement of any broken furniture or utensils. Court costs arising from the actions of inmates or his own creations were to be paid out of his own pocket. Any monies left at the end of his term of office were deemed his wages. He was responsible for providing the means and running costs of the inmates work, with any profits from this employment deemed his bonus. While this type of contract would have released the overseers from the day to day workload, and allowed a far better assessment of parish accounts, the devil would have been in the detail, for an over-generous contract would have left the parish out of pocket. Perhaps it was for this reason the contract was only an annual one.

It would seem the Pakenham overseer was not far off the mark. Other parish accounts suggest the going rate for a governor at this period of time was in the region of £50 per annum. (In 1790 the Boxford vestry was paying their governor £46 per annum[119]). By removing this from the £200, the Pakenham governor would be left with £150 to manage the workhouse and inmates, effectively £3 per week. As the capacity of Pakenham workhouse is unknown, working on the basis of the East Bergholt rate of 1/- to 1/6 per inmate[120], £3 would seem to be sufficient to cover up to forty inmates. While it is impossible to calculate the costs of all the overheads he would have had to meet, it was clearly within his own control to 'manipulate' the budget in order to ensure a satisfactory wage; with the proceeds of the work of the inmates an extra bonus. Inevitably the ones most at risk from this form of contract were the inmates themselves, though the parish officers had ensured they should receive the basic necessaries by inserting the vague clause *'and providing for the inmates good and sufficient lodging and clothing and also diet and provisions'*.

Another parish to use this method of remuneration was Hadleigh. When Robert Tiler took on the management of their workhouse in 1782, he agreed to provide, maintain and keep all men, women and children *with good wholesome proper and sufficient meals, drink, ... and other necessaries* from his own pocket. He also agreed to supply spinning wheels, spindles combs and combing pots for the employment of the inmates. His contract was calculated on the basis of 2/- per inmate[121].

Incentives were often included as a part of the contract. When Robert Buxton assumed the role of governor of Walsham le Willows workhouse in 1790 his wage was 11 guineas. A extra clause was added that if the committee felt his management had been productive he would be allowed a further guinea[122]. However it is possible this job was vacated within the year if this is the same person who took on the Pakenham role in 1791. The governor of Bradfield St George's parish workhouse found a more direct way of subsidising his wages. He charged the parish accounts 1s 3d every fortnight for baking and washing, with further infrequent amounts of 6s for beer for his wife[123].

Hiring and firing of governors was commonplace. A vestry meeting entry at East Bergholt on 4th November 1741 announced that John King should be removed from the workhouse, as soon as convenient, claiming he had not performed his duty as governor to the satisfaction of the town. Nevertheless it would seem he got a reprieve and was reinstated, for his widow assumed charge of the workhouse 'on his death' in 1743. Her reign was brief for she retired in 1747, to be succeeded by former inmate Susan Easterson who became an unlikely governess for about two years[124].

There are other instances of disagreements between vestries and governors or their spouses. Following the death in June 1792 of William Roberts, who had been governor of St Matthews Ipswich for just a year, his wife complained to the vestry, that she was unable to provide for the poor, requesting some redress for the loss she had occurred. It would seem she assumed some sort of role when her husband was instated as governor, for which she had received an allowance of 5/-. Since his death this had been stopped causing her a considerable loss. On considering the situation the vestry decided to allow her 5 guineas for the losses she had occurred. An order was also made for a weekly payment of 2/8d to be continued for the present time[125].

Advertisements for vacancies for governors and managers appear with regular frequency in the Ipswich Journal in the early nineteenth century. Nonetheless there was never a shortage of applicants for these quite lucrative positions. When a position became available at Hessett in 1805, within three weeks of placing the advert, the position had been filled with the appointment of Robert Dowsing. Equally the Hadleigh advert in February 1782 mentioned above was fulfilled by the appointment of Mr Tyler by early April.

Depending on the size of the workhouse, some additional regular staff would have been employed to help. The most obvious full time position in the house would have been the cook. He or she would have been responsible for the preparation of the set menus as drawn up by the parish officers. These were taken with regimental timing morning, noon and evening. In many of the houses, general household management would have been done by the inmates themselves, be it under the careful supervision of the governor, though charwomen might have been employed in the larger premises to carry out wash day activities.

No doubt the second most important position within the workhouse was that of a medic. The conditions within these buildings meant virus and disease were prevalent. An unchecked epidemic of a disease like small pox could quickly spread beyond the walls of the workhouse and out into the community at large[126]. Hence the services of a doctor or surgeon would be a must for any establishment. Again a contract would be drawn up for the medic/s either to serve just the inmates of the workhouse, or alternatively to care for the whole parish. The conditions of the agreement were normally on an 'as and when' basis, with the term of the contract again anything between one and five years.

From the Brandon Town book, we learn of the appointment in 1733 of Mr John Morris as physician, apothecary and surgeon *to attend the workhouse as necessary*. His remuneration for this commitment was: *"£6-10-0d yearly for his pains."* However it would appear the committee felt they did not get value for money as when Joseph Gibs took over the same position on 17th September 1736, he was paid just £5 for the following year[127]. At Fressingfield, during an outbreak of small pox in 1797/98, the overseer contracted Dr Girling and Dr French to inoculate the twelve inmates. For this they received several payments ranging between £4 14s 0d and £29 0s 0d[128].

Another profession in demand in some parish workhouses was that of school teacher. It was considered a prudent move by many to educate the children of the workhouse, though more emphasis was placed on reading than writing. This was deemed necessary to prevent inmate children having an advantage over those outside. Bearing in mind, there was little schooling available for poor children in the community. Even in the workhouses it would seem some put more emphasis on the subject than others. At Hadleigh in 1796 John Hart of the Alabaster school was called before the feoffees to explain why he no longer taught the children in the workhouse, as his agreement stipulated. Hart explained the reason was because the teaching accommodation in the building had been taken away ten years previously. He added he was more than happy to resume his duties if the accommodation were restored[129].

Because of the tight budgets these workhouses were run under, some vestries, particularly the smaller parishes, would include teaching within the governor's remit, rather than employ a separate person. This was particularly the case where a husband and wife ran the establishment. At Framlingham in 1699, the master of the poor house was *'everyday to give leave to each child two hours... to read, write or cast accounts as the school master think fittest'[130]*. In August 1791 at a general vestry meeting of St Matthews Ipswich one of the listed 'articles' for the better government of the poor stipulated the governor would teach the catechism to the children at least three times a week, on Sunday, Tuesday and Fridays, highlighting the status of religion at the time[131].

While not staff in the full sense of the word, 'craftsmen' would be employed within the production side of the workhouse. In 1731 Edmund Copping was contracted by Brandon workhouse committee to provide combed wool for the workhouse. Furthermore he was to teach those in the house how to spin, and provide all the necessary materials and equipment. He would then purchase the woven cloth back from the committee at a price comparable to that 'charged by Mr Bugg of this town'; and stand any losses from wasted materials. For all this he received one shilling a week from the workhouse committee and a further 2 shillings a month from the parish overseer[132].

Payments were on occasion supplemented with other perks. In 1664 John Kilborne agreed to provide wool to Framlingham workhouse for 300 poor people to spin. In return he was given a residence and a small salary[133].

============

Taken from: *Brandon Town Book, S.R.O.(B) FL536/7/1*

Here we have a recipe **'To make Oakam'** (Oakum), a preparation of tarred fibre used in shipbuilding, for caulking or packing the joints of timbers in wooden vessels.

This is followed by the **'Bill of Fare** (menu) **for ye Workhouse'**, dated 20 May 1729.

- Hasty Pudd(ing) = made of flour, milk and water to a consistency of batter.
- Neats Heart = the heart of an oxen or cattle

The footnote **'treacle on bread for such as can't eat cheese'**, highlights the rudimentary nature of a pauper's palate not used to eating such refined foods.

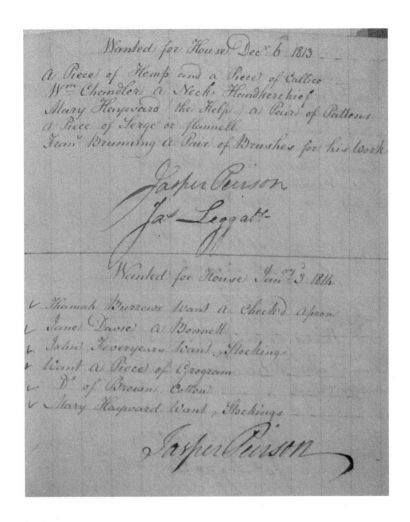

Taken from: *Memorandum of Requirements of the Workhouse; Framlingham Overseers Accounts. S.R.O.(I) FC101/G19/7;*

This volume records the requirements of the inmates of Framlingham workhouse, and **'Mary Hayward, the help'**. Items include clothing such as stockings, checked apron and a bonnet; and pieces of hemp and callico for their work. The signatures are those of the overseers.

Taken from: *The Ipswich Journal 23rd February 1782*

Here consecutive advertisements placed by overseers of Rattlesden and Hadleigh both inviting couples to undertake the care and management of the poor in their respective workhouses.

While Rattlesden state any applicant/s should be '**of good morals and character**', with a preference for a couple with no children; the Hadleigh overseer stipulate the successful applicant will be responsible for '**every necessary, except bedding and cloathing**', though the salary would be calculated '**at per head**' to include the basic costs for providing essentials.

Taken from: *Metfield Overseers Accounts FC91/G11/1*

Here we have a Surgeons agreement made between the parishioners of Metfield and Mr Rich(ar)d Priest, surgeon and apothecary of Harleston, Norfolk.

His basic salary of £6 per annum, supplemented for instances of small pox, broken bones and midwifery, plus **'no more than 3 shillings for each journey to any part of the parish'**.

Taken from: *Brandon Town Book S.R.O.(B) FL536/7/1*

This list of **'Furniture for the Workhouse'** at Brandon includes journeys to Methwold, Thetford and Milden(hall) demonstrating the sort of distances an overseer would cover in search of those basic goods and chattles required to stock a workhouse..

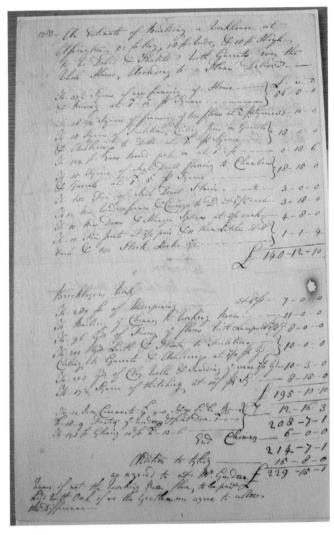

Taken from: *Assington Building costs, S.R.O.(B) FL521/7/10,*

Here we have 'The Estimate of Building a Workhouse at Assington 52 ft long, 18 ft wide, & 15 ft high to be Dobed (daubed) & Thatched With Garrets over the Whole House According to a Plan Delivered'.

Part of: *Fire Insurance policy 1803; & premium receipts for Groton workhouse 1789-1826; S.R.O.(B); FL506/7/38;*

For insurance cover of £200 in 1803, an annual premium of six shillings was made, with a further four shillings tax duty.

The summery sheets for the eight year period 1818 to 1826 show how the premium rose and fell.

Taken from: *Hadleigh workhouse 'Contract Book' 1789-1809;*
S.R.O.(B); FB81/G1/1;

This page gives detail of contracts between the overseers and churchwardens of Hadleigh, and Edward Cooper as the meat supplier of good steer beef and wither mutton, and Abraham Reeve as provider of flour **'equal in quality to samples already provided'**.

Chapter Five

EMPLOYMENT

Palgrave

With the concept of the workhouse being the provision of employment for those unable to support themselves, one of the primary decisions the various parish vestries had to make was the type of work to be carried out in their house. In Suffolk the main industries had always been agriculture, textiles and fisheries, thus it was these industries which formed the basis of workhouse employment.

By requiring the parish officers to provide '*a convenient Stock of Flax, Hemp, Wool, Thread, Iron, and other necessary Ware and Stuff, to set the Poor on Work*' the original 1601 Act identified the textile industry as the principal occupation for any inmates. The fact there were several elements within the spinning process, which could be done either individually or in groups would have made this an ideal type of employment for the parish workhouse. Equally as the work could be carried out within the workhouse it removed the issue of inclement weather hindering the operation as in the case of the agricultural industry.

There would have been plenty of textile experience in the dole queues in Suffolk throughout the period of the parish workhouse. In the thirteenth to fifteenth centuries many of the county's towns and villages, particularly in the south-western corner, had prospered from the manufacture of the 'old draperies' like worsters and broadcloths. However by the beginning of the seventeenth century this industry was in sharp decline, putting hundreds if not thousands of 'skilled workers' in need of relief[134].

While this demise would seem to have been partly offset by the emergence of the new draperies industry in the seventeen and early eighteenth centuries, the fact it established itself along the Waveney valley meant little benefit was felt by the parishes affected by the demise of the old draperies. And anyway by the end of the 1700s this had suffered a similar fate.[135] Now it was the hemp and flax spinners and linen weavers who trod the path to the overseer's door.

Typically it was the women and children who were involved in the spinning process; the skills involved having been passed down from one generation to the next. First the raw product had to be harvested, and steeped to produce a pliable material. This was then cleaned, combed, and carded before being passed on to the spinners who sat at their wheels, plying their distaff, producing the yarn. This in turn was passed on to the weaver, in all probability another family member, to be woven into cloth ready for manufacturing into garments and merchandise. Thus when the market for the end product ceased,[136] it had a domino effect on the whole chain of family members. The loss of a market for the weaver meant no work for the less skilled but equally important carders, spinners etc.

Parish vestries would have been aware of these skilled 'assets' of their inmates, hence in order to be competitive they would seek out governors with experience in either the production or sale of their targeted 'trade'. When Haverhill advertised for a new governor in 1813, they stipulated any one applying should have a broad understanding of the sack industry[137]. Equally part of the contract Robert Tiler agreed with the overseers of Hadleigh involved him supplying spinning wheels, spindles, combs and combing pots for the employment of the inmates[138]. In 1824 Clare vestry proposed to Mr Webb of Haverhill that he should teach the inmates the art of spinning carded wool at the workhouse[139].

Another type of textile produced along the Waveney valley was that of oakum. Otherwise known as Jute, it was the product of an annual plant, grown to harvest in a matter of three to four months. Following a process which involved steeping the cut stems in warm water for a period of time, (Brandon overseer insisted this should not be scalding hot water); the now supple stems were plaited into water-proof ropes[140]. These were mainly used in the fishing industry for plugging cracks and small holes in the fishing boats. The whole process played havoc with an inmate's hands, so much many would become scarred for life as a result.

As mentioned above Suffolk has always been chiefly an agricultural county. From the period when the Anglo Saxons set foot on its shores, farming has provided employment for the highest percentage of the population. Being a labour intensive industry, there was always plenty of menial work for the labouring classes, where numbers were more important than any level of skill. Therefore any adverse effect on the industry, like inclement weather or national depression, would be quickly felt in the local community. This would inevitably increase the length of the queues at the overseer's door. With agriculture being almost totally an outdoor activity, any work provided for the inmates had to be taken on the farms themselves.

The daily routine would be for the inmates to be transported to the farms early in the morning, spend the day working the fields, only to return to the house for evening meal and bed. The type of work inmates would undertake could be hand weeding the freshly germinating crops, scaring birds off the spring wheat, or picking stones off the fields. Inside work where available might include strawing out the cattle sheds, or some maintenance around the buildings, especially if the 'inmate' was a capable tradesman. At harvest time boys would spend days on end in the barns gleaning the corn with their flails.

Stones picked from the fields were used on another outdoor task often given to inmates. At this period of time a parish was responsible for the upkeep of roads and turnpikes which ran through its community. Gangs of labourers were employed to maintain these byways. The stones picked from the fields would be transported by horse and cart, to the byways where the labourers, with their sledge hammers, picks shovels and rammers at the ready would make good the roadways ready for the traffic of the day: general carriers, the parcel post, stage coaches and the like. The inmates at Fressingfield workhouse seemed to alternate the two jobs, 'ston pickin' one week, then 'rod mending' the next[141].

It was normally the women-folk and older children who did the field work of stone picking. The common practice was for a gang to be paid by the number of heaps collected, with a specific number of bucketfuls to make up a heap. An eagle eyed foreman or overseer would be capable of identifying if a heap of fifty bucketfuls was one short. In many cases the stones would be immediately carried away to where the roads needed repairing. However if crops were too forward to allow the horse and cart on the field without causing damage, this part of the operation would be put on hold until after harvest[142].

The vestry of St Stephen's Ipswich, identified a niche occupation for their inmates. Situated in the heart of the town, this parish was within striking distance of the borough's docks which sat on the river Orwell. One of the surplus products of the docks in the 1700s was coconut fibres. The overseer identified the opportunity of utilising this free commodity to make mats. Their accounts show that while spinning and knitting provided the largest regular portion of the income generated by their inmates; revenue in the region of 3/- a week was obtained from matt cutting[143].

These mats would have been woven by inserting tufts of coconut fibres through string warps suspended from beams. The tufts forming the piles of the rugs or mats. Other stages in the process involved mat trimmers who tidied the tufts and edges, and made good any small 'faults', and mat combers who straightened out any twisted strands of yarn and generally improve the overall appearance[144].

Another source of employment in the workhouse, would have been in the brewing room. With ale being the main form of liquor at this time, there would have been a demand for significant quantities. More often than not a room was set aside as a brewery, something evident in the many surviving inventories.

Here the process would begin the previous day, with the malt being left to steep overnight in a mash tub. Early the following morning the malt would be thoroughly mixed by hand, then transferred to a keeler which was raised on legs. A wilsh, (a sheath of wickerwork) was fitted over the keeler to prevent the grains from escaping. Boiling water was then added to cover the malt. Next the keeler was covered with a cloth, and left to steep. The mix would then be bulked up by the addition of up to twelve gallons of boiling water and then thoroughly stirred with a masher. After allowing this to stand for three to four hours the liquid would be drawn from the keeler into a mash tub. This gave off the first wort. Once cooled down a pint of yeast would be added to commence fermentation. Often a second wort would be made by adding more water to the malt left in the keeler. The resultant liquor of this second batch was known as 'small beer'. The beer would then be poured into hogsheads with the aid of a funnel, though in Suffolk this was known as a Tunnel. Hops were grown extensively throughout the county particularly around the Stowmarket area, where an annual hops fair was held in September[145].

Other work undertaken in parish workhouses included domestic chores. It would often be within the remit of the governor to ensure the house was kept in a clean and tidy condition. At Ipswich St Matthews, one of the house rules stipulated the house should be swept clean every day, then the beds be made and rooms to be swept every morning *'by such as shall be appointed by the governor.* It continues *the governor and such others of the family as are capable of assisting shall wash and clean the clothes and linen belonging to the inmates*[146]. This identifying the inmates as 'family' was quite commonplace throughout workhouse accounts and suggests a closely knit community existed within the premises.

Any commodities produced in the workhouse would either be for the use of the inmates or to be sold to generate income to help offset the costs of running the house. Obviously the amount generated would vary enormously, affected by a number of factors, inmate numbers, time of year, or efficiency of workhouse. Hadleigh was a market town which had thrived on the profits of the textile trade for some two hundred years. Towards the end of the eighteenth century income was generated by selling yarn spun by its inmates to Norwich weavers. The largest amount of £531 13s 8½d., achieved in the year 1796, could be partly accounted for by the arctic conditions experienced that winter. Equally doubling of the inmates numbers in the period between 1790 and 1809 mirrored the years of the napolionic wars[147]. At Fressingfield, a sizable village situated to the north of the county in the Waveney valley where the linen trade was in decline, a full capacity of thirty inmates generated an income of nearly £47 in 1802[148].

At Walsham le Willows, the monthly accounts for 1736 show the amounts of between 9/4d in February and 16/8d in December were received variously from: 'income from workhouse', 'spinning' and 'for yarn'. Although inmate numbers are not recorded, the fact there does not appear to be any significant variation between summer and winter receipts would suggest a fairly constant number of inmates[149].

The spinning wheel would, on most occasions have accounted for by far the biggest proportion of workhouse income. Other work would also contribute to the end figures. At Ipswich St Margarets, 'The Workhouse Book' divides the income into 'poor work', 'garden stuff' and infrequent amounts on 1s for 'grain', though the type of grain is not clarified. Whereas poor work brought in anything between £1 12s 0d and £2 10s 0d, the garden produce varied from just 7d to 2/1d. Any revenue from the latter would have been a bonus, bearing in mind the prime target of this produce would have been for the inmates and staff of the workhouse, thereby decreasing the burden the food bill would otherwise place on the parish purse[150].

In order to encourage inmates to be as productive as possible, some parish vestries would offer inducements to conscientious inmates. At Lowestoft the parish officers who drew up the rules included a clause 5 which stated that any inmate working more than their allotted hours was to be paid 'overplus' for their efforts[151].

Although the primary reason for workhouses was the creation of employment for the inmates, the very existence of the establishment would have created work for much of the local community. From the outset, vestries would have required professional advice on matters regarding the acquisition of the premises, and any subsequent construction or conversion work from people such as lawyers, architects, and other professions. We find evidence of this early involvement in the Brandon Town book where Mr A. Martin received 10/- for a 'deed of parish agreement'. James Martin, (possibly a relative) received 7/6 for his 'draughts and assistance' and John Snare received 10/6 for his 'measuring at the works'[152]. They would seem to have been the design / surveyor team. Elsewhere the churchwardens at Wetheringsett paid Mr Sicklemore 7d. **'being a surveyors rate for the Workhouse'[153]**.

Further down the Brandon accounts we find evidence of a number of tradesmen who carried out work on the house prior to its opening. Carpenter Thomas Willett received separate amounts of £4 12s 0d & £12 19s 2d for fitting windows and doors at the Workhouse. Thomas Tonyce, the local mason, received a total of £31 24s 5d for his skills. Local plumber Robert Millet carried out such work as laying lead water pipes in the property and the conduits to take the waste away. For this he received various amounts of £4 4s 0d & £7 5s 0d. Blacksmith William Browning could well have provided the carpenters from his home forged range of best quality or standard nails, be they batten, burnished, lead or 'standard by the price' nails. His bill for materials which he provided for the workhouse came to £14 14s 6d. [154].

Although the accounts do not quantify the amount of work undertaken by these tradesmen, a table in 'The Gentlemans

Magazine' of 1732 put the daily rate of craftsmen including carpenters, and masons at 1/2d per day[155].

These same tradesmen may well have benefited from the significant amount of ongoing maintenance required on these old cottage type premises. The various churchwardens and overseer's accounts are literally littered with examples of remedial work. At Helmingham in 1746 local thatcher James Sewil carried out some renovation work to the roof of the parish workhouse. For this he received £2 10s 3d. Whether his work was substandard, or perhaps he had hung up his leggatt and rake, and retired is unknown; but in 1753, a Thomas Gilbert received a payment of just 15/- for some patching work he had carried out to the premises. Both entries specified the material used as straw. This would have been a far cheaper but less durable option that the higher quality Norfolk reed which was used for thatching the more affluent houses and properties[156].

Local carters were one of those important but unnoticed operators in the local economy. The hauliers of their time, they would transport goods, equipment and even personel from one place to another. This would include the removal of paupers who fell on hard times back to their legal place of settlement. The likes of Peter Mallows and his family, as illustrated in a later chapter, would have been transported back to the perimeters of the parish which in effect 'owned' them. This often culminated with the pauper and / or their family being admitted into the workhouse. The diversity of the work of the carrier is demonstrated at Wetheringsett, where in October 1732 a carrier was paid seven shillings for '*removeing J Clakes family from the Workehouse and bringing them back again and fetching timber from Town lands*. Then on 8th November the same Overseer paid out 13 shillings for the '*carriage of 350 bricks to the town house, … and carrying Jno Clarke's goods from the workhouse and bringing Wid Kerry's & Martha Savage's back ...* Yet another instance saw a carrier receive three shillings for carrying three trees from Thomas Vinlsons to the workhouse, though whether these were to be used as fire wood or carpentry work is not stated[157].

Many of the county's workhouses would have had land attached to them. This would have been of significant benefit to all concerned. The primary usage of any fertile lands was either for the grazing of sheep or cattle primary for milk and butter, and ultimately meat; or to grow fruit and vegetables like potatoes, turnips cabbages, apples and pear trees or berried fruit such as raspberries and blackberries. All of this would have been of double benefit to the parish. Not only would it save on the expenses of the workhouse, but it also gave the inmates work experience and quite possibly a degree of self-satisfaction, something that would have bade them well when they were released.

The limited amount of expenditure required for items like seeds would be more than balanced out by income generated by the sale of any excess produce. Thereby providing a financial gain to help the overseers balance their books. The workhouse book for St Margaret's Ipswich shows in 1754 the governor ordered 8d worth of seeds for the garden in November, and then another 3/6d worth in January. While the later ones could have been the first spring crops, the November entry would suggest either these were for broad beans or shallots, which could be sown that late in the year. The account book shows the garden produce brought in anything between 1/10d to 7/6d weekly in the summer months, though this dwindled to zero in many of the winter months[158].

The Stansfield overseer's accounts for 1788 show that while spinning work brought in roughly 2/9d a week, potato sales were about 1/9d. Other 'work' entries of amounts in the region of 3/6d. bulked up the total income from workhouse sales for the following six months to £9 5s 4d. Set beside the income from the poor rates of £51 4s 6d for the same period, this shows that income from the workhouse accounted for one sixth of the income required to run this house[159].

Again there would have been work in the garden for the local community. At Friston, in March 1827 the parish accountant James Cooper made out a bill for ploughing work done at the workhouse[160]. The overseers accounts for Wetheringsett show in October 1740, sixteen shillings and six pence was paid for ditching done at the workhouse, a menial but very important part of rural husbandry[161].

With the two main tasks for an overseer being to find employment for those in the workhouse, while keeping the numbers inside to a minimum, it would be seen as a very prudent move to identify situations where an inmate could be released from the house and contribute to the well being of the community. Such an instant happened at Fressingfield, when former inmate Nicholas Algar was released, given a cart by the overseers, and then employed carrying out various carting and delivery work around the town. For this he received a wage averaging about 16/- a month. This included carting chaldrons of coal to the house[162].

On a more personal note the Fressingfield barber made regular trips to the workhouse to cut hair and give the male inmates a shave. For this he received one shilling a head, presumably metaphorically speaking, unless his name was Mr Todd![163].

As a final comment on the issue of workhouse employment; the ultimate annotation must rest with Thomas Etheridge, a carpenter of Fressingfield, Tom picked up regular jobs at the workhouse, such as in December 1797 when he repaired the workhouse stairs. For this he received 2/-. However it was in the winter of 1798 when his services were in the greatest demand. With the parish in the midst of a severe outbreak of small pox, he received regular orders for his coffins. These were priced at 9/- each for adults, with a child's size costing 3/6d.[164]

==============

Chapter Six

INMATES and CONDITIONS

Blaxhall

The Poor Law Acts of the late sixteenth century categorised the poor into three groups. The aged, sick and impotent who could not work; the idle poor who would not work; and the willing poor who could and would work were it available. These laws then empowered parish vestries to provide long term care for the first group in the community, either in their own homes, or in purpose build 'almshouses'. To the second group any 'help' would be confined to the House of Correction. It was to the third group which became known as *'the deserved poor'*; the legislation offered most assistance. It obliged parish vestries to provide the means to encourage this section back into the workplace, suggesting purpose built premises as an instrument of achieving this: i.e. The Workhouse.

Prior to 1722 the decision as to who was admitted into the workhouse fell mainly on the shoulders of the parish overseers; (the other route being through the local Justice of the Peace). It was they who evaluated which group the needy fell in, whether a pauper was unable to work, and hence eligible for 'out relief', or capable and thus met the requirements for admittance into the house. By no means all who fell with in the 'deserved poor' bracket would be admitted. The overseer would often decide that it was better to provide out relief be it in the form of clothing or food, rather than commit the family to the destitution and dependence of the workhouse. If a pauper could contribute to the maintenance or upkeep of the parish, then it was a better return to the parish to offer some relief in return for 'community work'. This would often keep both parties happy, to the pauper the workhouse was considered the last place on earth to visit, somewhere to avoid at all costs. While to the overseer and parish officers, the smaller the number of inmates in the workhouse, the less the cost of maintaining them from the parish poor rate.

However following the introduction of the 'workhouse test' with n the 1723 Act, which decreed that parish relief was only to be available to inmates, numbers in the workhouses grew dramatically. With more families forced into this reluctant lifestyle, conditions within the premises became more cramped and less bearable. A pauper family would do their utmost to avoid going to the parish for aid. They preferred to live meagre lives often surviving off the charity of those more able and willing. Even so, for many it was inevitable that they would ultimately end up incarcerated within the confines of these loveless places

In a mainly agricultural county like Suffolk, inmate numbers would fluctuate with the seasons. During the spring, when labourers were required to tend new crops, through to the harvest time, when it was a case of all hands to the fields and barns. For this reason a governor would find he or she had more inmates to cater for in winter than in summer. This variation can be seen from the inmate numbers recorded in various overseers' accounts. When a new governor took over at East Bergholt in February 1758 he was in charge of eighteen persons. During the following summer this fell to about a dozen, only to rise back up to eighteen in the following winter[165].

Poverty and therefore workhouse numbers could be affected by international events. The national depression which took place at the end of the eighteenth century, coupled with the effects of the Napoleonic wars resulted in a significant rise in the number of inmates across the country. At Fressingfield, between 1775 and 1802 the house constantly reached its capacity of thirty. It was not until 1810 that the numbers began to drop to single figures[166].

The capacity of a workhouse was based on conditions akin to the extremities endured by pauper labouring families. It was by no means uncommon for a working class family, consisting of ten to twelve hungry stomachs to be living in a tenement of one up one down arrangement. Sleeping head to toe, or even in shifts was by no means unheard of. The fact the capacity was calculated on these lines is borne out by figures given in a 1776 survey of the country's parish workhouses.[167] Set beside inventory detail, they show an average ratio of about four inmates per bed. An inventory of the workhouse at Wetheringsett gives a bed count of ten, while the survey states a capacity of forty[168]. Equally St Margaret's Ipswich, deemed in 1748, as the 'County Workhouse', boasted a capacity of one hundred in the survey, with inventories taken at the same time giving a bed count of between twenty and twenty-five[169].

So much for numbers. As to the type of pauper found at the overseer's workhouse door. Contrary to the popular believe that all workhouse inmates came from the poorest group of society, the category of 'deserved poor' would on occasion encompass people from many walks of life. Almost anyone could suddenly find themselves unable to support their family, and turn to the parish for aid for one of a number of reasons. Particularly in a rural county like Suffolk where the single largest factor affecting the numbers of people unable to find work was the weather. Agriculture and fisheries, more than any other industry have always been at the mercy of the elements. A bad winter or poor harvest would put thousands on the dole. And while the menial labourer accounted for the biggest part of those affected, it was by no means exclusive to this group.

With the three largest industries in the county, agriculture, fisheries and textiles, providing trade and employment for hundreds of ancillary businesses, blacksmith, butchers, tailors, and clothiers.

Any slump or depression on one industry would soon bring about unemployment and hardship throughout the community. Equally a breadwinner could find themselves without a job from an unforeseen direction, like illness or injury, a failed business. A devastating property fire was a common occurrence in the days of wood, plaster and thatched buildings, made even more inevitable when candlesticks were added to the mix. Any one of these catastrophes could leave a family destitute, and at the door of the Overseer

For the same reasons a workhouse could provide residence for inmates from any age group. From pregnant mothers and infant babies to the aged. Analysis of a census of the inmates at Long Melford taken in the early part of the nineteenth century can be used to provide a breakdown of the numbers[170]. From a primary figure of 126 inmates, approximately six per cent of the population of the town of 2068, as counted in 1811; *a figure no doubt fuelled by the Napoleonic wars*; we find seventy-two (57 per cent) were female. On closer analysis it becomes clear while the females ages ranged fairly evenly across the spectrum, the males were mainly either under twenty or aged and infirm. With only sixteen per cent of the males being of the working adults age bracket of twenty to fifty, at least thirty per cent of the females fell into the same group, showing it was the women and children who were more likely to be admitted. The male, normally the breadwinner, would be left in the community to re-establish himself in the workplace, when his wife and family would be released to join him.

Furthermore it is apparent that the Long Melford overseers adopted the policy of separating the sexes. A boy's room accounted for the majority of the teenage lads, while a drury room provided residence for most of the females in their teens and twenties. Equally the sick and infirm were segregated. A bedlam was set aside for the insane. Sixteen inmates were in the sick-room, twelve of whom were aged sixty plus. This type of division of inmates was something trumpeted by the newly created incorporations in their Houses of Industry.

In many cases there were members of the same family 'incarcerated' at the same time. The several instances of mother and child being confined together could be either cases as mentioned above where the father had remained in the community to fend for himself, with only the women and children getting the 'benefit' and relief of the workhouse. The alternative explanation being of illegitimacy. A single mother, unable to provide for her child would find herself, together with her offspring admitted into the house. The parish officers would then set about identifying the father. Once located he would be obliged, through court proceedings if necessary; to pay the cost of maintaining mother and child. In many cases this was enough to jolt the father into accepting his responsibility, thereby freeing the mother from the workhouse, and off parish relief.

An inmate's stay in the workhouse could be brief or extensive. A 'listings of the paupers in Framlingham workhouse' highlights this variation[171]. Between the months of June 1809 and December 1811 the overall numbers are remarkably constant between thirty five and thirty eight, with the lowest number of inmates of thirty three recorded in August 1809, and peaking at forty two in February 1810. While it is of no surprise the lowest numbers coincide with harvest time, the fact the workhouse had a capacity of 100, yet it appears only one quarter full at a time when the country was experiencing a severe depression is unusual. Over this 2½-year period some thirty-five paupers were admitted, a figure partly counterbalanced by sixteen being discharged back into the community. A further seven were either sent into service or apprenticeship, many within weeks of being admitted. Five deaths occurred in the house with just one birth. Eight cases of inmates 'absent without leave' with two females absconding on more than one occasion, prove this was not a place of choice. Some being caught by the local constables and returned, others vanished into the community.

A sad and poignantly brief stay was highlighted in these listings by a single entry in April 1810:- *Susan Potkin, admitted 20 March, died within 8 days, therefore the number in the family remains the same'*. This form of identification of inmates as 'family' is found elsewhere in workhouse records, including the vestry book of St Matthew's Ipswich. It demonstrates the camaraderie of those caught up in these establishments, and the desire of some overseers and vestries to be compassionate[172].

One of the elements of the old poor law was to ensure paupers were adequately clothed, with the overseer responsible for implementing this provision. In cases where an inmate brought in their own clothing, this would be recorded, in readiness for their discharge. On 21st January 1789 the Metfield overseer John Chapman recorded in his accounts detail of various wearing apparel stored in the workhouse chest, together with the owner's names. One cloak, one gown, one apron, one hat, and one pair of shoes and two stays belonging to Dame Warns while Widow Tiles had brought in with her two undercoats, two aprons, two white handkerchiefs, four pair of sleeves, one bib, one cloak and apparel of caps[173].

On other occasions a relative would provide clothing for an inmate, as in the case of William Reeder. When his wife was sent to the workhouse at Ipswich St Clements, he agreed to provide her with such clothes as the officers thought fit, and to pay the parish officers 2/6d a week while she was in the workhouse[174]. When all else failed the overseer would have to obtain any necessary clothing. In 1730 the Bildeston overseer purchased two pairs of shoes at 5/8d for John Walters then another pair at 1/8d for Ann Parker[175]. Joshua Kirby, the governor of Ipswich St Margaret's in December 1754 purchased a pair of shoes for Elizabeth Kitchen. He later arranged for a gown to be made for girl King for the princely sum of 1/6d. He had two more gowns, a shirt and a coat made for other inmates at a total cost of 3/8d.[176]

As a result of a 1697 Act of Parliament[177] paupers in receipt of poor relief were to have a capital P emblazon on their clothing, to signify pauper. Many parishes took this a step further by effecting a uniform for the inmates of a workhouse. At Framlingham in 1699, the children at the workhouse were to be clothed in blue with bonnets, '*like those at Christ Church Hospital in Ipswich*', and to have Robert Hitcham's arms upon their coats. In 1708 the governess, Ann Harding requested six boy's coats, six bonnets, two girls mantels and petticoats, two hanck[erchiefs], two capps(sic) and two aprons[178]. No doubt a local seamstress was then given the task of sewing the Hitcham coat of arms on, unless the governess did it herself. In 1791 the parish vestry of St Matthews, Ipswich instructed the governor that the boys in the house were to be clothed in a waistcoat and breaches, and the girls in a jacket and dress for work. The girls were to also have a decent dress for Sundays[179].

In 1742 the Brandon parish officers decided that *"Everyone receiving parish relief shall upon the right sleeve of their upper garment wear a badge with B. P. sewed on.* (Brandon Pauper); The penalty for any abuse of this was the withdrawal of all allowances, and the offender whipped. The same vestry meeting also ordered that all persons in the workhouse *do constantly attend divine service in their proper seat, and that all persons receiving collection do likewise attend divine service in the said seat and that the overseer do pay the collection after the divine service"[180].* This underlines the significant part religion played in the lives of inmates, throughout the existence of the workhouse, much as it did in everyday England. Sundays would have been the one occasion when many of the inmates saw the outside world. At Hadleigh, in the 1590's one half of the inmates were taken to church each Sunday morning, and the rest on Sunday afternoon[181].

Even where workhouses were farmed out, the overseer would retain the obligation to provide clothing. When the Hadleigh vestry advertised for a new governor in February 1782, they stipulated the successful applicant would be responsible for providing the inmates 'with all the necessary except for bedding and clothing'[182].

As explained the concept of the workhouse was one of a basic no frills regime. Conditions endured by inmates were orchestrated to act as a deterrent rather then to present any degree of comfort. Rules and regulations governed every aspect of daily life. Invariably once incarcerated within the workhouse, a pauper would remain within the premises throughout his period of confinement. The two exceptions being when inmates were sent to local farms or to attend divine service on the Sabbath as mentioned above. Morning and evening roll calls were orchestrated to ensure no one got a lay in, unless they could prove to be unwell or infirm. Meals were served from a set menu, chosen by the parish officers. The daily routines would ensure little if any free time.

Again we turn to the overseers records for detail of the workhouse regulations. The rules which were to be applied to the inmates at Lowestoft are set out in the overseers Town Book[183]. They define the military style routine of life within the walls. Every person was to work *'according to their ability'* between the hours of 7 a.m. and 6 p.m. between Lady Day and Michaelmas, with just an hour set aside for lunch. Because of the shorter daylight, winter hours were between 8 a.m. to 5 p.m. Another rule stated that anyone refusing to work, or attend church on a Sunday was to be punished by the forfeiture of all meals for a day. If the misdemeanour continued then rations of bread and water were to continue until justice be done. No inmate would be allowed to leave the house with out the permission of the governor *'upon any pretence whatsoever'*.

Elsewhere at Ipswich St Matthews, the hours were even longer. Here the summertime hours were 5 a.m. to 9 p.m. With breakfast being served at 7 a.m., the inmates would have had two hours to implement the fifth rule, being: that everyone in the family was to wash and make themselves clean before breakfast, with children having their faces and hands washed and their heads combed every morning. There was an interesting order made by this vestry in 1790. The governor of the house was ordered not to give any 'outdoor' relief to any pauper with a dog or dogs, instead if they requested relief they were to be admitted to the workhouse[184]. Presumably the thinking being it was not the parish's responsibility to keep dogs in the community.

For both economical and practical reasons the diet of the inmates in a parish workhouse was basic. While the meals were by no means adventurous, overseers would not want inmates to become weak and undernourished, and thereby nothing but a liability. Simple wholesome food was the order of the day. The menu for the paupers in Brandon workhouse consisted of three meals a day. Sunday began with a morning meal of bread and cheese, followed by beef for dinner. Monday saw the remains of Sunday's lunch turned into a beef broth for breakfast, with peas porage at midday. Tuesday began with a milk broth, followed by beef for lunch. This in turn meant beef broth for Wednesday breakfast then hasty pudding for lunch. Thursday was bread and cheese followed by peas broth, with Friday beginning with milk broth and followed by neats heart. Saturday began with beef broth followed by peas porage for lunch. Bread and cheese was served each evening before bed. A footnote allowed for treacle to be served 'for such as can't eat cheese'[185].

To get an idea of how much this would cost, in 1736 the East Bergholt overseer recorded the following groceries for use in the workhouse: 12 lb. of beef @ 2/6d; a leg of mutton @ 11d.; a neck of veal @ 1/-; a calves head @ 8d.; a neck of mutton @ 6d.; a sheeps head @ 4d.; a lb of suet @ 4d; pork from 2½ to 4d a lb.; 30 eggs @ 2/6d; bread @ 3d; a loaf; flour @ 1/5 a peck; a bushell of wheat @ 4/-; a bushell of rye, @ 3/-; a lb of cheese @ 2/-; a pint of butter @ 6d; a lb of butter @ 5d, or more; sugar @ 4d. a lb; soap @ 6d a lb.; lb of candle 5d.; lb of salt @ 1½ ; a bushell of malt @ 3/-; peas and beans @ 2d a peck or more; grinding a bushel of wheat @ 4d.; 8 bushells of coals @ 1/8. [186]

Although the East Bergholt overseer did not reveal how long these provisions would last, his Beccles counterpart did. Between 1754 and 1759 his records show the weekly cost of supplies for the inmates averaged about £2. In one week in December 1754 a total of £1 15s 5½d was spent. This included 3 bushel of wheat & grinding 11/3d, 2 stone 2 pounds beef 7/6d, a barroll[sic] of beer 6/-, 3 pints butter 2/6d, a pound Candles 7/-. On closer analysis the figures for 1755 shows the winter bill for produce and relief averaged £4 18s 3d, while the summer bill dropped to £3 17s 8d, reflecting the higher demand on the parish ratepayers in the winter months[187].

What is interesting is the high percentage of produce obtained from the local agricultural industry, both dairy and arable. Wheat, rye, flour and malt, peas and beans from the arable farming; while the dairy farmers would have provided the meats, cheeses, milk, and butter. Something equally apparent is the type of meat joints, most being the cheaper cuts like the heads and necks of the beasts. The inclusion of mutton rather than lamb is another sign of the thrifty purchases. Much of this would have been turned into stews dumplings and broths. The inclusion of candles in both lists highlights a necessity of a period before the advent of electricity

To calculate how far this amount of produce would stretch, we can turn to a survey carried out into the state of the poor in 1797 by F.M. Eden. This deemed the following proportions sufficient for four fresh dinners a week, plus eight 'spoon' breakfasts, and suppers. 2lbs of meat would be adequate for three inmates. Otherwise 1 pint of milk, 2oz rice, 2oz pork, 1 pint boiled pease, 3oz cheese, 1oz butter and 4lb 14oz bread per person. With this each pauper would be allowed 12 pints of beer a week rationed at one pint per meal. Thus the need for the hogsheads in the brewery[188].

As stated previously conditions within the workhouse were deliberately basic, nonetheless it is apparent vestries did take steps to ensure conditions were acceptable. At Walsham le Willows in 1763 a contingency of seven couples were delegated to make daily checks of the workhouse. Their subsequent entries in the overseer's accounts provide a glimpse of the needs and conditions endured by the inmates. Entries dotted throughout the diary showing the various requirements and incidents, some trivial, others serious. There are a number of entries like the one on 24th October *'for want of clothing'*, and *'various complaints for wearing apparel'*. Another regular entry was *'complaints for stockings and shoes'*. On 4th August Mary Game grumbled to Thomas Punchard *'against the butter & milk'* though it is not clear if this was due to the condition or lack of. It would appear bed linen was in short supply for a number of entries mirror the one which claim Mary Brooks was *in need of sheets and linen*.

However it is apparent some of these assertions were at the least mischievous if not devious. Following an inspection of some of the allegations recorded by the parish officers, the overseer R Taylor wrote: *'gentlemen we have examined the house and we find that those who complain that they have no lining* (linen) *more than they will own till we searched for them and when we found them they said that did not know they had them.*

Obviously living in such confinement there would be friction between the inmates and staff. An example of this occurred on 3rd February when a *'complaint of quarrelling and fighting, mother Windard and Blowers especially'* was recorded. Then on 3rd April a grievance was made to Ellis Pett against Rebecca Turner *'for misusing people in the house, swearing and saying the woman of ye house askd me for poison for her'*. Whether or not the examiners received payments for their efforts is unclear, though it is apparent from an entry in the diary on 3rd August their efforts were monitored. One of the overseers, Mr J. Taylor Hovell wrote: *'I would beg of you gentlemen inspectors not to write your names to the day when you are not thear[sic]'*.[189]

The conditions were such that most inmates were only too pleased to free themselves from the workhouse, many would request discharge as soon as they felt able to care for themselves. However for at least one, it would seem the workhouse became more of a home. In the mid 1740s Susan Easterson was a resident inmate of the East Bergholt workhouse. However when the governor of the house retired in July 1747, Susan subsequently took on the role of governess. This situation lasted for about two years. Then following the appointment of Peace Garwood as the new Governor in 1749, she remained within the house, now listed as one of just three inmates under his care. Susan was ultimately destined to spend her final days in virtual isolation, for in the period prior to her death in January 1755 she was the only inmate[190].

It would seem Susan's period of tenure as governess was not a straightforward one, for during her reign a somewhat disturbing event occurred. William Tredgett was frequently in trouble with the parish officers. So much so he had on occasion been locked up in 'The Cage', this being a temporary gaol within the parish. Also on more than one instance he had been sent to the Bridewell in Ipswich, only to be released back into the community where he would commit further crimes. Eventually it was decided to *'put him altogether under restraint'*. It was decided to build a structure within the workhouse yard where he would be secured. Mr Sawer a local builder was employed to construct the building in question. His bill for the work amounting to £3 0s 10d. A *'cheen and lock for Willm*

Tredget was purchased for 2/- at the same time. However it would appear William was not easily tamed, for the overseer's accounts show just over a week later, on 19th December *2 new locks for Tredget cost 3/-*.[191]

When Peace Garwood became governor the vestry ordered him to allow William Tredget one shilling a week for any work done. Following William Tredgett's death *'the little house that stand in the workhouse yard that Willm Tredget had for his lodgings'* was sold to Mr Coleman for £1 1s 0d; presumably the parish officers did not anticipate a repeat of the experience.

A similar case arose at Wingfield, when in 1789 Thomas Clark, was sent to Ipswich Gaol, having been found guilty of felony and horse stealing. Upon deliberating on his sentence, two of the county's Justice of the Peace together with the gaol's own surgeon Mr George Stebbings, judged Thomas to be insane. As a result it was ordered he was to be temporarily confined to Ipswich Gaol. A court order was then made for his removal to Wingfield, being proved as his legal place of settlement. Prior to his removal, an order was sent to the Wingfield overseers to make ready *'the strong room already fitted up for such persons in the parish workhouse there'*. Once ready the prisoner was to be escorted to Wingfield, where he was to be detained *'as long as such lunacy or disorder shall continue and no longer'*. So at least he was given the proverbial light at the end of the tunnel, though if he was ever released has not been identified[192].

Another workhouse incident that involved the law happened at Walsham le Willows in 1813. George Stone, one of the county's Justice of the Peace, sent instruction on 9th March to the constable of the parish to apprehend Mary Parker, a pauper at the workhouse. She was then to be summonsed to appear at The Greyhound in Hopton on Tuesday 23rd March at eleven o'clock to answer the complaint brought about by Richard Gapp, churchwarden of Walsham le Willows that she did *'abuse and ill treat William Bainslaw, governor of the said Workhouse'*[193]. The outcome of the meeting is not recorded.

==========

Chapter Seven

SOME INMATE'S STORIES

Framlingham

As explained earlier inmates arrived at the workhouse door from many walks of life. For some it was a temporary measure, possibly following a piece of misfortune, while they got their lives sorted out. For others it was a way of life. The following examples illustrate the varied circumstances of families or individuals who experienced life on the inside of Suffolk's parish workhouses. In the first case Peter Mallows, a person seemingly on the fringes of the criminal world, found himself and his family incarcerated in Framlingham workhouse for a decade. And here incarcerated would definitely have been how it felt for this workhouse was situated within the castle walls, where once Mary Queen of Scots had sought refuge in her bid to hide from her sister Elizabeth.

The second case centres on James Jacques, a Bedfordshire soldier, who put himself forward to serve his country anticipating a fight with the Irish or French. Instead he found himself in a neighbouring English county, and through the inabilities of the British army to pay its soldiers a regular wage, unable to provide for his family. This resulted in him having to plead with the local overseer for support. A move which saw him and his family experience a temporary stay in the same workhouse, while the bureaucracy of the poor law cleared the route for him to return to his homeland.

The third story is an unproven narrative found in a booklet edited in 1869, entitled 'Ipswich 200 years ago'. It tells of the experiences of a former inmate of one of the borough's parish workhouses, whose life fluctuated like the tides of the Orwell. Thanks initially to the benevolence of the parish overseer who gave him one shilling to get him off his back. Whether true or not, it demonstrates how an individual's life could turn on the generosity or malevolence of others.

....

The Mallows of Framlingham

Following their marriage in the parish church of St Michael in 1790, Peter & Elizabeth Mallows had lived in Framlingham where Peter worked as a local labourer picking up work wherever he could. Theirs was a typical working class family of the period, with Elizabeth experiencing regular pregnancies, often followed by an infant death. It would seem Peter found himself in a spot of bother. Shortly after the birth of son Robert in 1801, he took his family and moved to the parish of Nayland, where for what ever reason he felt it necessary to adopt the pseudonym of Peter Bloomfield. Was he running away from something or someone? Presumably trying to create a new life for him and his family, what is apparent is things did not go according to plan.

Initially it would appear Peter and his family settled into the area, Elizabeth conceived two more children during their stay in Nayland. However it is apparent by 1808 Peter had become destitute with no employment or anywhere for his family to live. With a wife and five children to support, it was not long before he found himself in need of relief from the overseer.

Seen from the overseer's viewpoint, providing help for a family of this size would have presented a considerable drain on the rate-payers of Nayland. He knew he had no legal obligation to support this family, instead he made it a priority to seek out their legal place of settlement. In the meantime the whole family would have experienced the 'hospitality' of the former Guildhall, now Nayland's parish workhouse.

Following an appraisal of Peter's circumstances, it became apparent he and his family belonged to Framlingham. As Peter was not in possession of a settlement certificate acknowledging this fact from the Framlingham overseers, the Nayland counterpart had to apply to the county court for a removal order. Once the overseer had the required form duly signed by the Justices of the Peace, he was able to arrange for the removal of the Mallow family out of his parish, with any costs incurred being passed on to the Framlingham vestry.

The journey back to Framlingham either on foot or at the best in the back of a carrier's cart, would have taken nearly two days[194]. Now Peter found himself, his five children, and his wife carrying an unborn child under the 'care' of the Framlingham Overseers. Because of Peter's circumstances, the Framlingham overseer's only option was to commit them to the local workhouse. Their stay proved to be a long one. Peter and his wife Elizabeth were to remain incarcerated in the castle workhouse until June 1818 when they were finally discharged back into the community. For the children the incarceration was not such a long one.

They were each put into apprenticeships with local businesses or families. Daughter Deborah was the first to leave when she was sent into the service of a Mr Aldrick in October 1810. Though the reason is unclear she did briefly return to the house for a month the following year, before being returned to Mr Aldricks care the following January. November 1812 saw Peter junior sent into the service of Mr Paynes and then four years later his younger brother Robert was apprenticed as house servant to Charles Chubb a gentleman of Framlingham. But for young Robert the painful story continues. Before he reached his fortieth birthday he had been declared a lunatic and become a patient at St Audry's, the mental institution at Melton. Ironically this had originally been the House of Industry for the Loes and Wilford district, until it was unincorporated in 1827 and converted into the County Asylum. Robert was to spend the rest of his life within this building.

Whilst in the workhouse the Mallows regularly appeared in the parish overseers *'memorandum of the requirements of the workhouse'*. This provides a glimpse of the sort of life the Mallows and their fellow inmates experienced in the workhouse. Many of the entries relate to the need for clothing and bedding. On 4th October 1813 Peter & Robert Mallows along with John Keer were each *'in need of a hat'*, while John Deaks required a pair of stockings. In May 1813 Peter Mallows required a neck handkerchief, then the following November he was in need of an under waistcoat. At the same time Sarah Brunning wanted a check apron, and Richard King a jacket. In September 1813 'Old Brown' was in need of a pair of breeches. Other requirements the overseers noted included brown cotton, a piece of calico and a piece of duffle for clothing. And a new chamber pot!!

The memorandum was compiled monthly by the overseers of the town. It shows their term of office was normally for a period of twelve months. Occasionally officers held the position for a longer period. Jasper Peirson officiated continuously from May 1813 to January 1815. Other overseers in this period were James Leggat and George and William Edwards.

Finally released in June 1818 along with his wife, it would appear Robert's period of confinement had taken its toll on his health. Like so many who experienced the stresses and stains within the workhouse, his life fell far short of the biblical three score years and ten. Proof conditions within the house were not conducive to good health is borne out by his untimely death within twelve months of his release. Peter died at the age of fifty seven and was laid to rest in St Michael's churchyard[195].

....

James Jacques of Bedfordshire

The Mallow's story demonstrates the role of the parish workhouse as a long term abode for the destitute in the seventeenth and eighteenth centuries. Another instance which happened in Framlingham shows how the workhouse could also be used as a temporary place of refuge. Back in October 1800 James Jacques, a soldier from Bedfordshire, found himself and his family 'camped up' in the Castle workhouse. Born in Bedfordshire c1770, he had begun his working life in 1789 as a servant to a local farmer in the little parish of Streatly. Within twelve months he had enlisted into the militia to serve his country. He signed up with the 12th Foot Bedfordshire Regiment. No doubt he would have been expecting a posting to Ireland where the 12th was currently in active service, though it unclear whether he did cross the Irish sea.

By 1795 the 12th regiment having returned from Ireland, was now deployed to Framlingham in Suffolk. Whilst in service there James met and married local-lass, Sarah Sayer. They began a family in the parish. The fact the British Army at this time was notoriously bad at paying it's soldiers would provide a perfect explanation why James found himself destitute. Unable to maintain his wife Sarah and two sons, the youngest just six weeks old, he sought parish relief from the Framlingham overseers.

As with the Mallows, the Jacques found themselves confined to the local workhouse while the overseer conducted his investigation into James' circumstances. In the same way as his Nayland counterpart, he was keen to keep the list of parish dependants to a minimum. When James' case was presented to the local J.P. Temple Chevallier, it was clear from his story the parish responsible for his upkeep was back in Streatly, Bedfordshire. The necessary papers were then duly signed by the J.P. and handed to the Framlingham overseers who then made arrangements to return him and his family back to Streatly where they lived until James death in 1832 with his wife Sarah surviving him by just three years[196].

....

Jacob Dedham, 'a traveller'

The third narrative can be found in a booklet written in the mid Victorian period concerning events which had happened some two hundred years previous. Though unsubstantiated it tells of a former inmate of the parish workhouse of Ipswich St Mary at the Elms. How the life of a pauper could be affected by those whose path he happened to cross, from the benevolence of the overseer who gave him a shilling to set him on his way, to the expectations of the nobility for whom he worked. From the pleasures bestowed on him by a wife of a foreign land, to those who sought to see him return to the baseness of life which had began his journey.

"The name of this person was Jacob Dedham, alias Caulius, who it appears was many years ago an inmate of the workhouse of this parish. Being of a restless and roving disposition and possessing considerable natural ability, he became a source of much anxiety and trouble to the authorities, and at last they started him off with one shilling in his pocket to try his fortune with the world. He made his way to London and got engaged on board some vessel going to the East Indies. On arriving out there he seems to have worked himself into notice and was at one time employed as a spy under Lord Cornwallis. He afterwards married a widow of a very rich nabob, and enjoyed every luxury, but he had many enemies around who conspired to ruin him and ultimately he was compelled to leave his wife and flee the country. He managed to reach England and one morning he was found lying in the porch of St Mary at the Elms church. He was taken before the magistrate, and would have been committed as a vagrant, but no one believed the marvellous story which he told. But Mr Bacon of Ipswich heard of it, and believed the man's story was true, he interceded on his behalf, and got a subscription raised for him, and Dedham lived in Ipswich for some time after that, obtaining on account of his sketching powers, a decent livelihood as an artist"[197].

A man who enjoyed the extremities of life!, or someone with a very adventurous mind?.

============

Chapter Eight

THE FINAL DEMISE

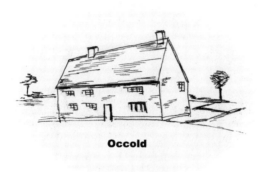

Occold

The demise of the parish workhouse took effect over a period of time, and for a number of reasons. The Guild Hall at Hadleigh remained in operation throughout the life of the parish workhouse but the majority had a far shorter lifespan. In some cases, vestries would choose to close their establishment, be it on financial grounds or through lack of available premises. A small community would often find the ever-spiralling cost of maintenance of the premises unsustainable, let alone the wages of the governor. When a building became uninhabitable through dilapidation, if alternative premises could not be acquired, a vestry was left with the one option. that being to return to the provision of out relief for its paupers.

Towards the end of the eighteenth century, a number of new initiatives were introduced, in an effort to combat the growing problem of unemployment and hardship. Often instigated by concerned local gentry and other parishioners, schemes adopted included a weekly distribution of flour, the provision of a family with clothes, or even supplementing a labourer's wages. These were aimed at providing relief for the needy in their own homes rather than sending them to the workhouse[198].

Ironically it was in the detail of the 1722 Act of Parliament, by recommending the amalgamation of parishes to run a single more efficient workhouse, which proved to be the downfall of the parish workhouse. The introduction of the House of Industry in the second half of the eighteenth century effectively began the demise. These large incorporations capable of holding up to 500 inmates, proved that by spreading the overheads of poor reform they could provide a more cost effective regime. Something of benefit to the vestries, parish officers, and rate paying public. Where these new buildings became available inmates were 'rehoused' from the locally run parochial workhouses into these massive establishments, often situated twenty to thirty plus miles away. Parishes which fell under the umbrella of these all-inclusive premises, now found they had redundant workhouses on their hands.

Vestries affected by these incorporations were now confronted with what to do with the superfluous buildings. Following the opening of the Samford House of Industry in 1766, a parish meeting took place at East Bergholt on 26th December 1768, where the vestry committee *"unanimously agreed to sell the workhouse, which is become useless to the said parish because the Union house at Tattingstone has been provided to serve for the whole district."* The churchwarden of the parish Mr Lewis soon found a buyer for on 16th April 1770, following approval by his vestry, he sold the old parish workhouse to Thomas May for £5.[199] Not all vestries were this swift to act. Holbrook, another parish affected by the opening of the Samford House of Industry, did not sell their 'now redundant' workhouse until 1802. However it would appear the delay was a shrewd move for it fetched the princely sum of £20.[200]

Other parishes affected in this way included the four parishes of Coddenham, Stonham Aspal, Helmingham & Barking which fell within the catchment area of the Bosmere and Claydon Incorporation when it opened in 1766. The opening of Cosford House of Industry situated at Semer, in 1780, tolled the death bells for the parish workhouses at Hitcham, Brettingham, Preston, Bildeston, Monks Eleigh, Lindsey, Kersey, Polstead, Aldham, Elmsett, and Lavenham. Stowmarket and Combs were both swallowed up by the Stow Incorporation which was established the same year.

Not all parishes which fell within the catchment areas joined these newly formed incorporations. In a few cases, vestries decided to remain independent. Hadleigh chose not to join the Cosford House of Industry, while Dunwich stayed outside the Blything equivalent. Also it would appear Woodbridge retained their independence when the Loes and Wilford Incorporation was set up in 1764. A decision justified when this incorporation was dissolved in 1827, with the House of Industry building being converted into the first county asylum. A move which meant the parishes within the two hundreds found themselves once again independently responsible for their own poor.

The introduction of these incorporations would have led to more direct comparisons of the two systems between the parishioners of the affected areas. Cosford House of Industry had proved the concept of a combined establishment worked. It was reported to be *'productive in the shortest space of time, of more beneficial effects than any other in the county'*[201]. It helped reduced the debt of the Cosford Incorporation from £8000 to just £180 in twenty years. Something which must have given the vestry at Hadleigh a few headaches, especially when in 1787, they required £126 to cover alterations to their workhouse. With income amounting to just £45, various loans totalling £59 had to be borrowed to make up the shortfall[202].

Although these incorporations took over the management of the poor of the parishes within their catchment area, there was still far more parish vestries in the county which continued on an independent basis. Of the one hundred and seventy nine known Suffolk parishes which adopted these workhouses, only the nineteen identified above were directly affected by the incorporations. However of those which retained a parish workhouse at the end of the eighteenth century, it is apparent from the 1803 and 1815 parliamentary reports, another fifteen ceased to operate during this period. This included the parishes of Groton, Shimpling, Horringer, Drinkstone, Brundish, Wilby, and Horham[203].

The final downfall of the parish workhouse was the introduction in 1834 of the New Poor Law Act[204]. Dissatisfaction with the whole system of poor relief had become a major issue in the 1820s. The more influential gentry felt the ever-increasing amount of poor rate required to offset parish relief was unacceptable. There was also considerable disquiet and unrest amongst paupers, largely brought about as a result of the rising costs of foodstuff, coupled with the lack of any increase in a labourer's wages. This was particularly noticeable in a rural environment like Suffolk. In 1832, in an attempt to combat this unrest, the government appointed a Royal Commission to examine the whole system of poor relief[205].

The resulting report, published in March 1834, made over twenty recommendations. The main one being that any parish relief available to able bodied paupers should be limited to those resident in 'well-regulated workhouses'. These were places where inmates *may be set to work according to the spirit and intention of the 43rd of Elizabeth*. It further recommended that regional unions, which encompassed all parishes, should be created for the management of their own poor. Each union was to have its own Union House, which would be run in such a way *as to be less desirable than that of the residence of an independent labourer of the lowest class.* A series of Acts of Parliament followed, implementing most of the recommendations, thereby effectively ending the existence of the parish workhouse[206].

With the concept of the parish workhouse confined to the history books, many parishes now found themselves with redundant buildings on their hands. For some, the state of the premises meant demolition was the only option. At Beccles a new Union House was built on the lands which had previously been occupied by the parish workhouse[207]. Of course not all buildings were in this condition, many, particularly the newly built ones were structurally sound and seen by the parish officers as an asset for the town.

However, under the rules of the new regime, before a parish could sell its workhouse, it had to obtain authorisation from the newly formed Poor Law Commissioners or P.L.C. The procedure being the parish officers would apply through their own union, to the P.L.C. The application form, which covered all parish properties, required full detail of the location, structure and condition of the property, together with any legalities concerning the potential sale[208].

An application dated 4th April 1837 drawn up by the churchwardens and overseers of Kettleburgh, and addressed to the Plomesgate Union, identified two parish properties they wished to sell. They also requested permission to demolish the workhouse, with the intention of selling off the materials for the benefit of the parish. As the property had been built on charity land, consent of the charity's trustees had already been obtained. Equally as the land was copyhold, approval of the Lord of the Manor had also been gained. A subsequent response from the P.L.C. dated 12th May 1837 gave permission for the sale of the two cottages, though it fails to make any judgement on the workhouse proposal which was presumably dealt with by a separate communication[209].

If the Kettleburgh officers met with the same response as their counterparts at Clare, when they requested permission to sell their workhouse, they may well have regretted their unbeknown honour of becoming the final vestry to construct a parish workhouse in Suffolk just ten years earlier.

The vestry of Clare had seen the advent of unification as an opportunity to sell their workhouse to help offset the losses the parish had incurred in repairing its church. They had applied through the Risbridge Union for authorisation from the P.L.C. to allow them to sell their workhouse and use the monies to *'offset the liquidation of the debt'* incurred in the said repairs. However the P.L.C. refused the application citeing that *'it was more expedient to use the building for Union purposes'*. Following a series of communications including one from the parish vestry containing the signatures of 150 of the parishioners; the P.L.C. partly relented by allowing the sale to go ahead. However it ordered that the money raised should be put towards refurbishments at Risbridge Union house at Haverhill. Eventually the sale took place with £500 being obtained. The dispute over what the money was to be used for continued over the coming months with more correspondence between the Commissioners and the parish officers. Eventually it was concluded that after various expenses were taken out, a sum of £36 9s 9d was to be spent on refurbishments at Haverhill. A further £180 was to pay outstanding bills to contractors Hephes & Chates, who had erected an infirmary and vagrants wards at Haverhill. The remaining monies were to be invested in '3% consolidated Bank Annuities' for the benefit of the parish[210]. Other parishes which sought conveyances to sell their properties at this time include: Groton[211], Kenton[212], Leiston[213], Rattlesden[214], Stonham Aspall[215], Sudbourne[216], and Whepstead[217].

It would seem one way to avoid this lengthy procedure was to return the property to its previous usage. The parish officers at Edwardstone decided to convert their workhouses back to their former identity as town houses for the benefit of their own paupers[218]. After Saxmundham fell under the umbrella of the Plomesgate Union, the workhouse cottages in Rendham road were converted back into accommodation for the poor[219]. A subsequent sale of the furniture and equipment from this workhouse raised £23 10s 9d[220].

The parish officers of Glemsford rented out the pastures which had belonged to their workhouse for £4 per annum, with the monies raised handed out to the paupers of the parish[221]. Equally the workhouse cottages at Great Glemham, together with twenty two acres of arable lands were let out to provide an annuity for the benefit of the parish. This was later used to repair the church of All Saints[222].

Elsewhere former workhouse buildings were converted and updated to provide some of the county's first national schools. At Woodbridge an agreement was drawn up in 1844 to allow part of the rooms in the old workhouse to be used as an infant school[223]. The previous year Brandon had successfully applied to the P.L.C. through the Thetford Union to convert the old workhouse into a National School. A deed dated 10th June 1843 reads: *"We, the guardians of the Poor of the Thetford Union ...with the consent of the Poor Law Commissioners and a majority of the ratepayers and owners of property in the Parish of Brandon, do freely ... grant and convey to the Minister, Churchwardens and overseers of the said Parish of Brandon, all that two storey house known by the name of the Old Workhouse ... for the purpose of ... a school for poor persons in the said Parish of Brandon and for no other purpose whatever."*[224]

Although the concept of the parish workhouse died with the birth of the New Poor Law Act of 1834, here in Suffolk a few of these buildings still exist at the end of the twenty first century. While their interiors and living conditions will no doubt have been upgraded to meet modern standards and requirements, their framework remain as a monument to times long past when the comforts of the 'inmates' were far more basic than those enjoyed by their twenty first century counterparts. Let us not forget the path of our predecessors. But for their experiences, ours would not be so smooth.

===========

18th century village scene

While it is surely beyond the capacity of the modern mind to fully appreciate the conditions endured by those paupers, the words of one of our county's most respected poets of the period, George Crabbe of Aldeburgh 1754-1832 gave an illuminating insight into that world.

Theirs is yon house that holds the parish-poor,
Whose walls of mud scarce bear the broken door;
There, where the putrid vapours, flagging, play,
And the dull wheel hums doleful through the day;--
There children dwell who know no parents' care;
Parents, who know no children's love, dwell there!
Heart-broken matrons on their joyless bed,
Forsaken wives, and mothers never wed;
Dejected widows with unheeded tears,
And crippled age with more than childhood fears;
The lame, the blind, and, far the happiest they!
The moping idiot and the madman gay.

Here too the sick their final doom receive,
Here brought, amid the scenes of grief, to grieve,
Where the loud groans from some sad chamber flow,
Mix'd with the clamours of the crowd below;
Here, sorrowing, they each kindred sorrow scan,
And the cold charities of man to man:
Whose laws indeed for ruin'd age provide,
And strong compulsion plucks the scrap from pride;
But still that scrap is bought with many a sigh,
And pride embitters what it can't deny.

Say ye, oppress'd by some fantastic woes,
Some jarring nerve that baffles your repose;
Who press the downy couch, while slaves advance
With timid eye, to read the distant glance;
Who with sad prayers the weary doctor tease,
To name the nameless ever-new disease;
Who with mock patience dire complaints endure,
Which real pain and that alone can cure;
How would ye bear in real pain to lie,
Despised, neglected, left alone to die?
How would ye bear to draw your latest breath,
Where all that's wretched paves the way for death?

Such is that room which one rude beam divides,
And naked rafters form the sloping sides;
Where the vile bands that bind the thatch are seen,
And lath and mud are all that lie between;
Save one dull pane, that, coarsely patch'd, gives way
To the rude tempest, yet excludes the day:
Here, on a matted flock, with dust o'erspread,
The drooping wretch reclines his languid head;
For him no hand the cordial cup applies,
Or wipes the tear that stagnates in his eyes;
No friends with soft discourse his pain beguile,
Or promise hope till sickness wears a smile.

But soon a loud and hasty summons calls,
Shakes the thin roof, and echoes round the walls;
Anon, a figure enters, quaintly neat,
All pride and business, bustle and conceit;
With looks unalter'd by these scenes of woe,
With speed that, entering, speaks his haste to go,
He bids the gazing throng around him fly,
And carries fate and physic in his eye:
A potent quack, long versed in human ills,
Who first insults the victim whom he kills;
Whose murd'rous hand a drowsy Bench protect,
And whose most tender mercy is neglect.

George Crabbe

==========

Chapter Nine

SUFFOLK'S PARISH WORKHOUSES

The 1776 National Survey of Parish Workhouses has provided the basis of the following list. However there are two apparent anomalies in the original listings. It double lists the parishes of Laxfield & Edwardstone. It correctly identifies them in their respective hundreds, but in both cases the second entry gives a conflicting capacity to the first, allowing for the conclusion that two additional parishes have been inaccurately named. Other sources used in compiling the following list include surveys in both 1803 and 1815, and references identified in general parish chest records such as Churchwardens and Overseers accounts.

To explain the symbols used:
<1776-1822> means in operation from before 1776 until after 1822;
1803> - 1815> means opened after 1803 until after 1815.

Acton;	1803> - 1815>	
Aldeburgh;	<1759 - 1776>	Capacity = 15
Aldham;	<1776 - 1780:	Capacity = 20
Alpheton;	<1776>	Capacity = 35
Assington;	<1776 - 1822>	Capacity = 20
Athelington;	1776> – 1803>	
Bacton;	1776> – 1803>	
Badingham;	1776> – 1814>	
Barking;	1728 – 1766:	
Barnardston;	c1747 - 1776>	Capacity = 30
Barrow;	<1776>	Capacity = 30
Barton Mills;	1776> – 1835	
Beccles;	<1754 – 1757>	

Bedfield	<? – 1834	
Belton;	<1776>	Capacity = 3
Benhall;	1776> – 1819>	
Bildeston;	<1776 – 1780:	Capacity = 30
Blaxhall;	1776> – 1834:	
Boxford;	<1764 – 1790>	Capacity = 30
Boxted:	1776> - 1822:	
Bradfield Combust;	1776> - 1803>	
Bradfield St George;	1776> - 1803>	
Brampton;	<1776>	Capacity = 10
Brandon;	1728 – 1820>>	Capacity = 21
Brettingham;	<1776 – 1781:	Capacity = 20
Brockley;	1776> - 1803>	
Bruisyard;	1776> - 1803>	
Brundish;	1776> – 1803>	
Bungay:-		
- Holy Trinity;	<1776>	
- St Mary;	<1776>	Capacity = 25
Bures St Mary;	<1776>	Capacity = 50
Bury St Edmunds; -		
- St Mary;	<1639 - 1793>	
- St James;	<1639 - 1797>	
Carlton;	1803> - 1815>	
Cavendish;	<1758 – 1820>	Capacity = 30
Chevington;	1776> – 1839:	
Chillisford;	<1805>	
Clare;	<1757 - 1836>	Capacity = 30
Cockfield;	<1776>	Capacity = 30
Coddenham;	<1761 – 1766:	
Combs;	<1776 - 1781	Capacity = 36
Cotton;	1776> – 1803>	
Cowlinge;	1776> - 1819>	

Cransfield;	1803> - 1815>	
Cratfield;	<1759 - 1776>	
Dalham;	<1776 - 1836:	Capacity = 14
Debenham;	>1653 - 1776>	Capacity = 40
Dennington;	c1606 - 1803>	
Denston;	<1776>	
Drinkstone;	1776> – 1803>	
East Bergholt;	c1734- 1763:	Capacity = c18
Edwardstone;	<1776 - 1810>	Capacity = 40
Elmsett;	<1776 – 1780:	Capacity = 12
Eye;	1593 - 1794	
Farnham;	<1776>	Capacity = 6
Felsham;	1803> - 1815>	
Fornham All Saints;	1776> - 1803>	
Framlingham;	c1653 - 1836>	Capacity = 100
Framsden;	<1776 - 1817>	Capacity = 40
Fressingfield;	<1775 - 1847	Capacity = 30
Friston;	1776> - 1813>	
Gedding;	1803> - 1815>	
Gislingham;	1803> - 1815>	
Glemsford;	<1776 - 1811>	Capacity = 50
Great Cornard;	<1776 - 1811>	Capacity = 20
Great Glemham;	1776> - 1830>	
Great Wratting;	1747- 1776>	
Great Waldingfield;	1776> - 1803>	
Groton;	<1776 – 1803>	Capacity = 30
Hadleigh;	1577 – 1835	Capacity = 100
Hartest;	<1776 - 1825	Capacity = 30
Hawstead;	1776> - 1803>	Capacity = 30
Haverhill;	<1776 - 1848:	Capacity = 40
Helmingham;	<1753 – 1766:	
Hepworth;	1776> - 1803>	

Hessett;	<1805>	
Hitcham;	<1776 – 1780:	Capacity = 30
Holbrook;	<1763:	
Hopton, by Thetford;	1776> - 1803>	
Horham;	1776> - 1803>	
Horringer;	1776> - 1803>	
Hoxne;	<1776–1835;	Capacity = 40
Hundon;	c1747–1805>	Capacity = 20
Iken;	1803> - 1815>	
Ilketshall St Margaret;	<1776>	
Ipswich :-		
- St Clements;	c1698-1836;	Capacity = 70
- St Helens;	<1776 - 1803>	Capacity = 10
- St Lawrence;	1738 - 1776>	Capacity = 25
- St Margarets;	1721 – 1836:	Capacity = 100
- St Mary Elms;	1746 - 1776>	Capacity = 10
- St Mary Quay;	<1776 – 1812>	Capacity = 25
- St Mary Stoke;	<1776>	Capacity = 30
- St Mary le Tower;	1731 – 1837:	Capacity = 30
- St Matthews;	1729 - 1836:	Capacity = 30
- St Nicholas;	<1776 – 1836:	Capacity = 20
- St Peter;	<1760 – 1830>	Capacity = 28
- St Stephens;	1731 - 1830	Capacity = 24
- Whitton / Thurston;	<1776- 1836	Capacity = 6
Ixworth;	1776> - 1803>	
Kelsale cum Carlton;	<1776>	Capacity = 40
Kenton;	1776> - 1836:	
Kettleburgh;	<1837>	
Kersey;	<1776 – 1780:	Capacity = 30
Lavenham;	<1776 – 1836:	Capacity = 80
Lawshall;	<1776>	
Laxfield;	<1776>	Capacity = 30

Leiston;	? – 1840:	
Little Bradley;	<1776>	
Little Cornard;	<1776>	Capacity = 14
Little Glemham;	1776> - 1803>	
Little Whelnetham;	1776> – 1837:	
Long Melford;	c1713 - 1801>	Capacity = 150
Lowestoft;	1739 - 1766?	
Mettingham;	<1776>	Capacity = 12
Mendham;	<1776 - 1803>	Capacity = 20
Mendlesham;	c1714 – 1776>	Capacity = 30
Metfield;	<1776>	Capacity = 30
Mildenhall;	1720-1834	Capacity = 70
Monks Eleigh;	<1776-1834	Capacity = 15
Mutford;	<1776>	Capacity = 10
Nayland with Wissington;	1734-1784>	Capacity = 40
Newmarket;	1776> - 1803>	
Newton;	<1776>	Capacity = 24
Occold;	1776> - 1803>	
Orford;	<1776 >	Capacity = 20
Pakenham;	1776> - 1803>	
Palgrave;	<1776>	Capacity = 30
Parham;	1776> - 1803>	
Pettaugh;	<1776>	Capacity = 15
Polstead;	<1776 – 1780:	Capacity = 30
Preston;	<1776>	Capacity = 16
Rattlesdon;	<1741 – 1854<	Capacity = 26
Redgrave;	photo	
Redlingfield;	1776> - 1803>	
Rendham;	1776> - 1803>	
Ringshall;	photo	
Rougham;	1776> - 1803>	
Saxmundham;	<1776 – 1835	Capacity = 60

Shimpling;	1776> - 1803>	
Snape;	<1776>	Capacity = 20
Somerleyton;	<1776>	Capacity = 3
Sotterley;	<1776>	Capacity = 14
Southwold;	<1739 - >?	
Sproughton;	c1707 – 1779	
Stanningfield;	1803> - 1815>	
Stansfield;	<1787 - 1815>	
Stoke Ash;	<1805>	
Stoke By Clare;	<1776-1801>	
Stoke by Nayland;	<1746 – 1837:	Capacity = 40
Stonham Aspal;	<1776 – 1807	
Stoven;	<1776>	Capacity = 6
Stowlangtoft;	1776> - 1781:	
Stowmarket;	<1777 – 1781:	Capacity = 85
Stowupland;	<1776 – 1781:	Capacity = 20
Stradbroke;	<1776>	Capacity = 40
Stradishall;	c1747 - 1776>	Capacity = 16
Stuton;	?	
Sudbourne;	<1776 - 1854	Capacity = 16
Syleham;	1776> - 1803>	
Tannington;	1803> - 1815>	
Thorndon;	1776> - 1844	
Thurston:	<1780 – 1832	
Tostock;	1776> - 1803>	
Tunstall;	<1803- 1827>	
Walpole;	<1776>	Capacity = 6
Walsham le Willows;	<1735-1784>	Capacity = 20
Wattisfield;	1776> - 1803>	
Westhall;	<1776>	Capacity = 10
Wetheringsett cum Brockford ; 1730 - 1776>		Capacity = 25
Whepstead;	1776> – 1839:	

Wickham Brook;	c1747-1834:	Capacity = 42
Wickham Skeith;	1776> - 1803>	
Wilby;	1776> - 1803>	
Wingfield;	1757 - 1803>	
Woolpit;	1776> - 1803>	
Worlingworth;	<1776- c1840	Capacity = 35
Woodbridge;	c1668 – 1835:	Capacity = 100
Wortham;	<1776 –1818>	Capacity = 30
Yaxley;	1777 - >?	

==========

Harvest time

90

REFERENCES and SOURCES

Abbreviations:

S.R.O. = Suffolk Record Office, **(I)** = Ipswich; **(B)** = Bury; **(L)** = Lowestoft
E.A.M. = East Anglian Magazine
E.A.D.T. = East Anglian Daily Times
S.F.H.S. = Suffolk Family History Society
F.B.W.E.A. = Fressingfield Branch of the Workers' Educational Association
Ipswich Journal 28 Aug 1813, p3 [3] = date of publication, page no, [column no]

Bibliography;

Dymond D. & Martin E., *An Historical Atlas of Suffolk*, (The Northgate Press Ltd, 1988)
Dymond D. & Northeast P., *A History of Suffolk*, (Phillimores 1985)
Jones W.A.B., *Hadleigh through the Ages*, (E.A.M. Ltd. 1977)
Langley M. & G. *At The Crossroads*, (Johnson of Nantwich Ltd. 1993)
Mingay C.E. *The Skilled Labourer*, (Longman Group Ltd, 1979)
Mingay C.E., *The Village Labourer*, (Longman Group Ltd, 1978)
Paterson T.F. *East Bergholt in Suffolk*, (Private 1923)
S.F.H.S., *A century of a Suffolk village, Fressingfield, 1750-1851;* (F.B.W.E.A. 1977)
Smedley N., *Life & Tradition in Suffolk & Essex*, (Aldine Press, 1976}
White, William, Whites *1844 Directory*, (David & Charles 1970)
Andrews, S. & Springall. T, Hadleigh and the Alabaster family; (Andrews & Springall. 2005);ISBN 1 874593 99X

Chapter One

[1] A.H.Dodd, *Elizabethan England*, (Book Club Associates 1974) p. 166
[2] *Statute of Cambridge (12 Rich.II c.7)*
[3] Langley, *Crossroads*, (1993), p. 1
[4] *The Roaming Beggar Act'* of 1564
[5] 1597 Act, *Act For the Relief of the Poor* (39 Eliz. c.3)
[6] 1601 Act; *An Acte for the Reliefe of the Poore* (43 Eliz. I c.2)
[7] Jones. *Hadleigh*, 1977, p.85
& Robert Malster, *A History of Ipswich*, (Phillimore & Co, 2000), p. 123
[8] Blackwood, *Tudor & Stuart Suffolk*, (Carnagie Publishing 2001) p.19
[9] Blackwood, *Tudor & Stuart* (2001) p.20
[10] Hearth Tax 1674
[11] Andrews & Springall, *Hadleigh*, (2005); p.299
[12] 1722-3 *An Act for amending the Laws relating to the Settlement, Imployment, and Relief of the Poor alias Knatchbull's Act*
[13] Mingay, *Village Labourer*, (1978), p. 96
[14] http://www.workhouses.org.uk/
[15] *An Abstraction of returns by the overseers of poor;* Session papers 31 (1776)
[16] Mingay, *Village Labourer*, (1978), p. 169
[17] Dymond & Martin, *Atlas (*1988). p. 96
[18] Dymond & Martin, *Atlas (*1988). p. 96
[19] Overseers Workhouse Acc; S.R.O.(I); FC110/G5/1
[20] Dymond & Northeast, *Suffolk*, (1985). p. 93

[21] F.M.Eden; State of the Poor 1797
[22] 1834 New Poor Law; *An Act for the Amendment and better Administration of the Laws relating to the Poor in England and Wales 1834*

Chapter Two
[23] *Henry Tooley, merchant of Ipswich, 15 March 1553;* PROB 11/36
[24] John Webb, *Poor Relief in Elizabethan Ipswich,* S.R.S. 1966, Intro p. 11
[25] Andrews & Springall, *Hadleigh,* (2005); p.260
[26] Andrews & Springall, *Hadleigh,* (2005); p.75
[27] Clive Paine, *The History of Eye,* Benyon de Beauvoir, 1993
[28] Dymond & Martin, *Atlas,* (1988). p. 96
[29] Paterson, *East Bergholt (*1923); p. 146 footnote
[30] Earl Stonham, *Overseer letter 1622;* S.R.O. (I) FB23/G4/1
[31] Aldeburgh *Borough Letter book 1625-1663;* S.R.O.(I) EE1/01/1/115
[32] Framlingham, ED file 1950; & *Town Book,* S.R.O.(I) FC101/A2/1
[33] Lowestoft *Town Book; 1616-1898,* S.R.O.(L) Acc283/1, p. 75v
[34] *ffeoffment of Vernon's charity* S.R.O.(B) FL638/11/1
[35] *Magistrate's Warrant* S.R.O.(B) FL506/7/33
[36] Groton deed: 1616; John Winthrop, lord of manor to churchwardens & overseers. S.R.O.(B)FL506/11/8
[37] Dymond & Martin, *Atlas* (1988). p. 96
[38] Dymond & Martin, *Atlas,* (1988). p. 58
[39] Robert Tiler agreement S.R.O.(B) K2/4/1
[40] *Photo The Old Workhouse,* S.R.O.(B), 1511/161/23
[41] *Photo of Guild Hall then workhouse,* S.R.O.(I) K626/1/145/23
[42] Barking *Vestry Minute Book,* S.R.O.(I), FB15/A1/1
[43] http://www.workhouses.org.uk/
[44] Deed of inter alia Guildhall/workhouse; S.R.O.(B) FL614/2368/9/7/5
[45] In 1834 Chadwick became secretary to the new Poor Law Commission. which oversaw the operation of the Poor Law Amendment Act between 1834 and 1846. Chadwick was largely responsible for devising the system under which the country was divided into groups of parishes administered by elected boards of guardians, each board with its own medical officer. http://www.victorianweb.org/history/chad1.html
[46] Aldeburgh *Borough Letter Book;* S.R.O.(I) EE1/01/1/115
[47] Cowling *Overseers Accounts 1805-1817;* S.R.O.(B) FL556/1/1
[48] *Henry Tooley, merchant of Ipswich, 15 March 1553;* PROB 11/36
[49] John Webb, *Poor Relief in Elizabethan Ipswich,* S.R.S. 1966, Intro p. 12
[50] Dymond & Northeast, *Suffolk,* (1985). p. 77
[51] White 1844, *(1970),* p. 207
[52] White 1844, *(1970),* p. 559
[53] Long Melford *Estimation for workhouse extension;* S.R.O.(B) FL509/7/16
[54] Polstead, *Workhouse Lease, 1746;* S.R.O.(B) FB78/G13/1
[55] Wingfield, *Overseers Agreement 1757;* S.R.O.(I) FC84/G10/1
[56] Monks Eleigh, *Causton & Baker Charity feoffment* S.R.O. (B) L607/11/26
[57] *Estimation and receipt for building workhouse* S.R.O.(B) FL521/7/10
[58] *Lowestoft Town Book; 1616-1898,* S.R.O.(L) Acc283/1, p. 75v
[59] www.brandon-heritage.co.uk
[60] Parham *loan agreement for workhouse construction* S.R.O.(I) FC110/G5/4
[61] Kettleburgh, *Overseers Bundle of papers relating to workhouse sale* S.R.O.(I) FC109/G10/1
[62] Assington, *Use of blacksmith shop as workhouse c1778;* S.R.O.(B) FL521/7/43
[63] Irvine Read; *Christmas Day in the Workhouse;* F.F.H.S. web site 2006
[64] *Carlton Hall estate map* S.R.O.(I) HB441/A/36
[65] Saxmundham, *papers relating to workhouse sale,* S.R.O.(I) HA519/324

66 Friston, *tithe map/1841 census data*
67 Parham, *deed relating to finances to build;* S.R.O.(I) FC110/G5/1
68 Dennington, *Goldings and Sowgates site in Dennington* S.R.O.(I) FC112/L1/4
69 Monks Eleigh, *Causton & Baker Charity feoffment* S.R.O. (B) L607/11/26
70 Stonham Aspel, *Sale of property used as workhouse* S.R.O.(I) FB22/C11/7 & 8
71 Barking *Vestry minute Book* S.R.O.(I) FB15/A1/1
72 Brandon *Town Book,* S.R.O.(B) FL536/7/1
73 Wingfield *Overseers Acc* S.R.O.(I) FC84/G10/1
74 http://www.brandon-heritage.co.uk
75 Ips St Mathews *Vestry Book 1790-1820,* S.R.O.(I) FB95/A3/1

Chapter Three
76 Brandon Town Book, S.R.O.(B) FL536/7/1
77 Andrews & Springall, *Hadleigh,* (2005); p. 105
78 Jones, *Hadleigh,* (1977), p. 33
79 Sudbourne *Overseers Acc & Dis;* FC169/G1/3
80 Metfield, *Overseers Inventories* S.R.O.(I) FC91/G6/6
81 Ips. St Mary Elms, *Overseers Acc 1760-1777,* S.R.O.(I) FB104/G1/2
82 Clare, *Overseers notebook inc inventory,* S.R.O.(B) FL501/7/129
83 Cratfield, *Overseers Accounts* S.R.O.(I) FC62/G5/1
84 Wetheringsett, *Churchwardens Acc 1732-1741,* S.R.O.(I) FB151/G15/1
85 Haverhill, *Inventory of Workhouse Furniture 1813* S.R.O.(I) FL578/1/4
86 Saxmundham, *Overseers Accounts 1794-1843,* S.R.O. (I) FC137/G1/1
87 Helmingham, *Churchwardens Accounts 1745-1932,* S.R.O.(I) FB46/E1/1
88 Wetheringsett, *Churchwardens Acc 1732-1741,* S.R.O.(I) FB151/G15/1
89 Redlingfield, *Churchwardens Acc 1824-1837,* S.R.O.(I) FB134/G2/1
90 Orford, *Chamberlains Account 1713- 1767,* S.R.O.(I) EE5/5/1
91 Wetheringsett, *Churchwardens Acc 1730-1743* S.R.O.(I) FB151/E5/3
92 Stoke by Nayland, *Constables Accounts,* S.R.O.(B) FB80/I1/2
93 Ips. St Margaret, *Land tax;* S.R.O.(I) C/1/9/4/1/1
94 Ips. St Matthew, *Land tax;* S.R.O.(I) C/1/9/4/1/9
95 Ips. St Matthew, *Land & Window tax;* S.R.O.(I) C/1/9/4/3/4
96 Ips St Lawrence 1779, *Land Tax 1799,* S.R.O.(I) B150/11/1 (1-2)
97 Walsham, *Overseer Acc 1785-1790,* S.R.O.(I) FL646/7/2
98 Orford, *Chamberlains Account 1713- 1767,* S.R.O.(I) EE5/5/1
99 Ips. borough water rents, *Borough Water Rentals ;* S.R.O.(I) C5/5/6/5
100 Brandon, *Town Book,* S.R.O.(B) FL536/7/1
101 Worlingworth Ins, S.R.O.(I) FC94/G10/2 & 1808, G10/3
102 Hepworth Ins, *Overseers misc papers* S.R.O.(B) FL582/7/15
103 Stoke by Clare Ins, *Fire Insurance 1795,* S.R.O.(B) HA517/D19
104 Groton Ins, *Fire insurance policy 1803;* S.R.O. (B) FL506/7/38
105 Occold Fire; *Ipswich Journal 8 March 1800 p3 [3]*

Chapter Four
106 Knatchbulls act
107 Ips Journal index, S.F.H.S. various dates, Ipswich Record Office.
108 Bury, *Ipswich Journal 23 Feb 1782, p.3.(3)*
109 Debenham, Ips Journal, 13th July 1765.
110 Hadleigh, S.R.O.(B) K2/4/1
111 Ips St Margaret, *The Workhouse Book 1754-1760,* S.R.O.(I) FB93/G5/17

[112] Paterson, *East Bergholt, (*1923); p. 143
[113] Boxford, *Bundle of parish agreements* S.R.O.(I) FB77/G1/6/1 &/6/3
[114] Hadleigh and the Alabasters p. 260
[115] Saxmundham, *Overseers Accs 1794-1843;* S.R.O.(I) FC137/G1/1
[116] Dymond & Martin, *Atlas (*1988). p. 96
[117] Paterson, *East Bergholt, (*1923); p. 143
[118] Robert Buxton contract *1791;* S.R.O.(B) FL614/2368/7/10/1
[119] Boxford, *Bundle of parish agreement,* S.R.O.(I) FB77/G1/6/3
[120] Paterson, *East Bergholt, (*1923), p. 143
[121] Hadleigh, *Robert Tiler agreement* S.R.O.(B) K2/4/1
[122] Walsham 1790 wages, *Overseer Acc 1785-1790,* S.R.O.(I) , FI646/7/2
[123] Bradfield St George *'Poor Law in a Suffolk Village',* Rev J.R.M. Wright (ed), E.A.M. 1951-52; vol xi, p. 698-99
[124] Paterson, *East Bergholt, (*1923), p. 143
[125] Ips. St Matthews, *Vestry Book 1790-1820,* S.R.O.(I) FB95/A3/1
[126] Jones, *Hadleigh, (*1977); p. 86
[127] Brandon Town Book, FL536/7/1
[128] S.F.H.S., *Fressingfield,* 1977, p. 33
[129] Hadleigh, Jones, *Hadleigh, (*1977), p. 93
[130] Framlingham, *Town Book,* S.R.O.(I) FC101/A2/1
[131] Ips St Mathews, *Vestry Book 1790-1820,* S.R.O.(I) FB95/A3/1
[132] Brandon *Town Book,* S.R.O.(B) FL536/7/1
[133] Framlingham *Overseers Acc 1665;* S.R.O.(I) FC101/A3/2/32

Chapter Five

[134] Blackwood, *Tudor & Stuart* (2001) p.19
[135] Blackwood, *Tudor & Stuart* (2001) p.20
[136] Blackwood, *Tudor & Stuart* (2001) p.22
[137] *Ipswich Journal 28 Aug 1813, p.3 [3]*
[138] *Robert Tiler agreement S.R.O. (B); K2/4/1*
[139] Clare *Additional Accounts; 1823-1825,* S.R.O.(B) FI501/7/28
[140] Brandon *Town Book,* S.R.O.(B) FL536/7/1
[141] S.F.H.S., *Fressingfield,* (1977)
[142] George E. Evens, *Ask The Fellows who cut the hay,* Faber & Faber 1956, pp. 75-79
[143] Ips St Stephen, *Overseers Disb. 1731-1743,* S.R.O.(I) FB107/G3/1
[144] A Dictionary of Occupational terms; p398; The Open University, Cd
[145] Smedley, *Life and Tradition (*1976), p. 122
[146] Ips St Matthews, *Vestry Book 1790-1820,* S.R.O.(I) FB95/A3/1
[147] Jones, *Hadleigh,(*1977); p. 85
[148] S.F.H.S., *Fressingfield,* (1977)
[149] Walsham le Willows, *Overseer Acc 1785-1790,* S.R.O.(I) FL646/7/2
[150] Ips St Margaret, *The Workhouse Book,* S.R.O.(I) FB93/G5/17
[151] Lowestoft town book; Acc 283 (M18) /1; p77
[152] Brandon, *Town Book,* S.R.O.(B) FL536/7/1
[153] Wetheringsett, *Churchwardens Accounts* S.R.O.(I) FB151/E5/3
[154] Brandon, *Town Book,* S.R.O.(B) FL536/7/1
[155] The Gentlemans Magazine, S.R.O. (I) EG54-59
[156] Helmingham *Churchwardens Acc 1745-1932;* S.R.O.(I) FB46/E1/1
[157] Wetheringsett, *Churchwardens Acc 1730-1743;* S.R.O.(I), FB151/E5/3
[158] Ips St Margarets 1754 seeds; *The Workhouse Book,* S.R.O.(I), FB93/G5/17
[159] Stansfield *Overseers Accounts 1786-1802;* S.R.O.(B), FL627/7.1
[160] Friston 1827 ploughing; *'Bill for ploughing work',* S.R.O.(I), FC124/A3/664

[161] Wetheringsett *Churchwardens Acc 1730-1743* S.R.O.(I), FB151/E5/3
[162] S.F.H.S., *Fressingfield,* (1977), p.28
[163] Fressingfield, *Town Book 1797-1801,* S.R.O.(I), EG16/G1/3
[164] Fressingfield, *Town Book 1797-1801,* S.R.O.(I), EG16/G1/3

Chapter Six

[165] Paterson, *East Bergholt (1923),* p. 143
[166] S.F.H.S., *Fressingfield,* (1977) p.28
[167] *An Abstraction of returns by the overseers of poor;* Session papers 31 (1776)
[168] Wetheringsett, *Churchwardens Acc 1747-56,* S.R.O.(I), FB151/G15/2
[169] Ips St Margarets, *Rate Assessments:* S.R.O.(I), FB93/G4/3
& *Overseers Rates 1747/48,* S.R.O.(I), FB93/G4/1
[170] Long Melford *Kentwell Hall Estates* S.R.O.(I), HA505/3/67
[171] Framlingham, *Listing of Workhouse Paupers,* S.R.O.(I), FC101/G19/1
[172] Ips. St Matthews, *Vestry Book 1790-1820,* S.R.O.(I), FB95/A3/1
[173] Metfield, *Guardians of poor book 1788-1795,* S.R.O.(I), FC91/G11/1
[174] Ips. St Clements, *Wm Reader provision of clothing for wife;* S.R.O.(I), FB98/G9/3
[175] Bildeston, *Workhouse Book, 1730-1757,* S.R.O.(B) FB79/G4/1
[176] Ips St Margarets, *The Workhouse Book 1754-1760,* S.R.O.(I) FB93/G5/17
[177] 1697 Act; *Act For supplying some Defects in the Laws for the Relief of the Poor (8 & 9 Will II c.30)*
[178] Framlingham, *Overseers Accs 1706-1784,* S.R.O.(I) GB437/1/1 (Lanham Museum Archives)
[179] Ips. St Matthews, *Vestry Book 1790-1820,* S.R.O.(I) FB95/A3/1
[180] Brandon, *Town Book,* S.R.O.(B), FL536/7/1
[181] Jones, *Hadleigh,* (1977), p. 33
[182] Hadleigh, *Robert Tiler agreement* S.R.O.(B), K2/4/1
[183] Lowestoft, *Town Book; 1616-1898,* S.R.O.(L) Acc283/1, p. 77
[184] Ips St Matthews, *Vestry Book 1790-1820,* S.R.O.(I) FB95/A3/1
[185] hasty pudding = made of flour and milk or water, to a consistency of batter; *Oxford Dictionary*
& neats heart = the heart of an oxen or cattle; *Oxford Dictionary*
[186] Paterson, *East Bergholt,* (1923), p. 141
[187] Beccles, *Overseers Accs 1754-1759;* S.R.O.(L) 109/G1/3
[188] F. M. Eden – State of the Poor 1797
[189] Walsham le Willows *Overseer Acc 1785-1790,* S.R.O.(I), FI646/7/2
[190] Paterson, *East Bergholt,* (1923), p. 147
[191] Paterson, *East Bergholt, (*1923), p. 142-3
[192] Wingfield, *Overseers Accs Lunatics;* S.R.O.(I), FC84/G11/1
[193] Walsham le Willows, *Constable's Warrant for Mary Parker,* S.R.O. (B) FL646/9/10

Chapter Seven

[194] Mingay, *Village Labourer,* (1978), p. 75
[195] **Mallows documents**:
Framlingham *Parish Registers S.R.O.(I), FC101/D3/~*
Peter Mallows removal order; *Peter Bloomfield alias Mallow Nayland to Framlingham, S.R.O.(I) FC101/G9/5/40*
Deborah Mallows apprenticeship; *Listing of Workhouse Paupers, S.R.O.(I), FC101/G19/1*
Peter Mallows apprenticeship; *Listing of Workhouse Paupers, S.R.O.(I), FC101/G19/1*
Robert Mallows *Apprentice indent 1816; S.R.O.(I) FC101/G11/13/68*
+ *Conveyance of lunatic to Melton 1839; S.R.O.(I), FC101/G20/1/35*
Memorandum of requirements of workhouse; Overseers Accounts S.R.O.(I) FC101/G19/7
[196] **Jacques documents**

Settlement Exam; *S.R.O.(I), FC101/G9/5/85*
+ removal order *S.R.O.(I), FC101/G9/10/117*
IGI for Bedfordshire detail; *www.familysearch.org*
[197] **Jacob Dedham narrative**
Herbert Chamberlain, *Ipswich 200 years Ago*, E.A.D.T. c1889; pp. 50-51.

Chapter Eight

[198] Mingay, *Village Labourer*, (1978), p. 119
[199] Paterson, *East Bergholt, (*1923), p. 149
[200] *White 1844*, (1970); p. 255
[201] Jones, *Hadleigh*, (1977); p. 86
[202] Jones, *Hadleigh, (*1977), p. 81
[203] Dymond & Martin, *Atlas* (1988). p. 96
[204] 1834 New Poor Law; *An Act for the Amendment and better Administration of the Laws relating to the Poor in England and Wales 1834*
[205] Dymond & Northeast, *Suffolk*, (1985). p. 90
[206] *http://www.workhouses.org.uk/*
[207] *White 1844, (*1970); p. 417
[208] *http://www.workhouses.org.uk/*
[209] Kettleburgh, *bundle of papers relating to workhouse sale* S.R.O.(I), FC109/G10/1
[210] Clare, *Various papers relating to workhouse sale*, S.R.O.(B) FL501/7/138-151
[211] Groton, *P.L.C. correspondence re workhouse sale*, S.R.O.(B), FL506/7/39
[212] Kenton, *Sale Request to P.L.C.* S.R.O.(I), FB44/G4/1
[213] Leiston, *Vestry paper relating to workhouse sale*: S.R.O.(I), FC130/A1/1
[214] Rattleden, *Overseers papers relating to workhouse* S.R.O.(B), FL500/7/18
[215] Stonham Aspall; conveyance to bargain and sale of workhouse, 1807, S.R.O.(I), FB/22/C11/1
[216] Sudbourne, *bundle of papers relate to workhouse sale.* S.R.O.(I), FC169/G3/1
[217] Whepstead, *Conveyance of workhouse*, S.R.O/(B), FL651/13/9
[218] *White 1844*, (1970); p. 549
[219] *White 1844, (*1970); p. 171
[220] Saxmundham *Overseers Accounts 1794-1843*, S.R.O.(I) FC137/G1/1
[221] *White 1844, (*1970); p. 550
[222] *White 1844*, (1970); p. 163
[223] Woodbridge, *Agreement to let rooms in former workhouse as infant school;* S.R.O.(I), FC25/L8/1/7
[224] *White 1844*, (1970); p. 584

Act titles curtesy of *http://www.workhouses.org.uk/*
